I0759853

ART, CRAFT, COLOR

ART CRAFT COLOR

Brighten Your Life with Projects
in Every Color of the Rainbow

LISA SOLOMON

PHOTOGRAPHS BY ASHLEY LIMA

Hardie Grant

NORTH AMERICA

why hello

If you are looking at this page, then this book is for you.

Thank you for being a maker, a thinker, a believer, a seeker (or proxy to someone who identifies as something along those lines).

Because of you, the world is a bit brighter, aesthetic, and forever more colorful. Carry on.

(This book is also for D, my kiddo, my parents, and every friend, student, or even stranger I've had a conversation about art/craft/color with.)

CONTENTS

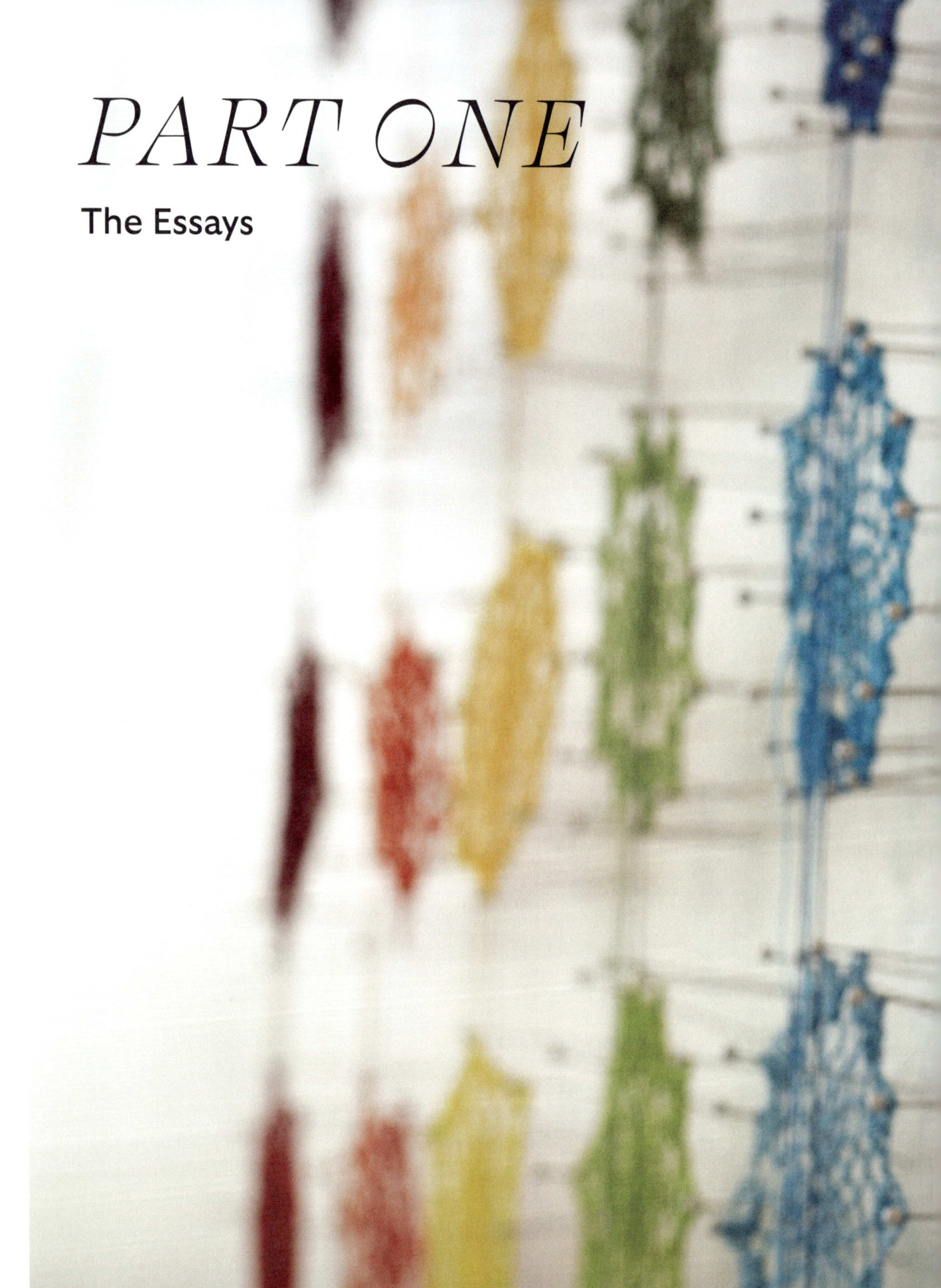

PART ONE

The Essays

ART, CRAFT

by Lisa Solomon

In all honesty dear reader, this is going to be messy. (Is it ok if I call you dear reader? Maybe it should be dear maker? Or dear crafter? Or dear artist? Or dear fellow maker/crafter/artist? This parenthetical right here is really just an inkling of how this all might go.)

No two ways about it. I've thought about the concepts of art *and* craft and art *vs.* craft my entire adult life. More seriously when I entered college and decided to get an art degree. This despite the uselessness that our surrounding culture—though thankfully not my family—seemed to think such a degree embodied. And then even more diligently when I went to get an MFA. Although by that time, I knew that studying and making art was indeed important—not just to me, but in a larger context of the world. And by then I was better prepared to research and tackle the ideas surrounding what honestly seemed to be a sort of arbitrary divide.

Thus, for the last thirty plus years I have had countless discussions about Art with a capital A and Craft with a capital C with artists, crafts-people, art historians, curators, and wannabe all-those-things. I've chatted with students—first fellow students and then my own students when I became a teacher. I've talked with professors—again, first my own professors as a student and nowadays my colleagues. I've discussed these ideas with people from all over the world. Heck, if a random person on the street approached me with this topic, I'd stop and converse. I've also read umpteen books and essays on said subjects. I've seen the concept tackled in exhibitions and watched more than a few youtubes, reels, posts across multiple platforms, and frankly whatever else has popped up in any given feed or was sent to me by friends, family, colleagues, and well-meaning strangers.

All of this is my very long-winded way of confessing that a significant amount of my own brain space has been dedicated to thinking about art and craft for a very long time. I've expressed my own shifting views—arguing to-and-fro with others about a multiplicity of interpretations of the word *art*, the word *craft*, and whether there is either no daylight at all, or else a giant chasm, between the two. In fact, I think on any given day I could probably be like a professional debater, playing devil's advocate and presenting either side of this discussion—with conviction even.

As I said, my own thoughts on the subject have vacillated—come to a fine point only to disperse again and emerge in a perhaps adjacent, yet none-the-less different locale. As I grow older, and I hope wiser, what I have come to believe is that I don't know. Nor do I actually *want* to have concrete and definitive definitions—about this, or any subject really—or the ability to put things neatly into a box.

Ideas and materials surrounding art and craft have been infused into my own art-making since I was an undergrad getting that potentially useless art degree in the early 1990s. My bourgeoning practice was informed by feminist theory and a desire to look past the European, white, male-dominated lens of art history. I sought to include imagery (domestic scenes), artifacts (dressmaking patterns), techniques (crochet and embroidery), and materials (thread and felt), that were often relegated to less than art-worthy status.

Throughout my career, I have also worked in many types of mediums—those typically assigned to fine art, such as oil painting, and those typically relegated to crafting, such as granny squares. I have attempted to cross pollinate my art with craft, and my craft with art. In fact, when asked about the grand art and craft debate, I often replied that I want my art to be craftful and my craft to be artful.

I tell my students that materials automatically lend themselves to preconceived notions. Thus, materials can inherently help to form the meaning behind a work. For example, if I say: "macaroni/pasta/dried goods painting," we most likely conjure up an image of something that could win a blue-ribbon at the state fair. Think: a portrait of Abraham Lincoln made with rigatoni and fusilli pasta, with a smattering of dried black beans to make up the bow tie and top hat. This is traditionally *not* something that would be considered fine art. But in the right setting, all these materials and the subject *could* be.

Let's try this again using glitter. Are we talking scrapbooking glitter on a swirly swoosh of sweet sixteen lettering, or an image of a winter wonderland where the glitter adds snow atop a picture

of our house? Or, perhaps, are we considering the artwork of Jamie Vasta, who uses glitter to create images that nod to the oil paintings of the Pre-Raphaelites. This is where ideas of context, irony, intention, the cannon of art history, and the maker's awareness of all of these, all come into play.

Western Art History

But if we're going to get into the weeds here, we need to know a little bit of basic Western art history. Prior to the Renaissance art and craft were more aligned. Not only were they in the same arena, they were simply not seen as being all that different from one another. Objects were created in ateliers and guilds where men and women performed the same tasks as one another. And these were tasks that were proclaimed valuable. The value was assigned by wealthy patrons—including royalty and the Church. Tapestries created by artisans lined the walls of the most important castles and the rooms of the most important people. These tapestries are now often housed in museums, and discussed in the terms that we use when discussing fine art (How do the formal qualities of these pieces work—the color, the composition, the scale?). Frocks embroidered by impeccably skilled people (again—both men and women) were worn by kings, queens, popes, and cardinals. Stained glass depicting biblical narratives were commissioned for all the churches so that the masses would know the stories.

These items were expensive—not for the every-person to have in their own homes. Their use was intended for the "greater good" which infused art with an importance that perhaps has helped to muddy the waters of our understanding throughout history. But that is a different discussion entirely.

Some have argued that we really need to pay attention to the patriarchal nature of the people and places that made these things. Because, though men and women both did the same artisanal art/craft work during this time, it was men who ran the businesses and houses that made these precious objects—and thus it was their work that was taken seriously and commanded respect.

Then the Renaissance came along, and it was painting, sculpting, and printmaking that became the main events in the fine art space. Embroidery and textiles, in particular, began to be the undertakings of women. These crafts were now seen less as a means for making a grand statement and more as utilitarian, functional. Perhaps still beautifully crafted, but no longer about the ever-important questions that art was addressing.

The subjects of art still included religion, but also portraiture of rich and important people, the depictions of historical events, and more. Artists who were akin to scientists (looking at you Durer and DaVinci) figured out how to depict 3D spaces on 2D planes. Perspective was no longer something you could only experience in person, but something that could be illustrated and understood by a viewer. The artist was now tackling concepts in the grand scheme of life! And castles didn't need elaborate tapestries to keep them warm anymore, so attentions were turned to the men painting chapel ceilings (Michelangelo), generating elaborate still lifes using the most expensive trade goods (Bruegel), tackling political uprisings (Goya), or elevating the quiet interior middle class domestic sphere—perhaps using a

It Ain't Fittin' to be Sittin', 2003, electrical wire + sound element (CD player, speakers, switch), 44 x 53½ inches wall piece, installed at Mills Art Museum, Oakland, CA

camera obscura to figure out how light actually works in the world (Vermeer).

Later, as the Western world entered the austerity of the Victorian Era, this divide between the making of beautiful but useful things and the importance of fine art only seemed to widen. The domestic arts fell under the purview of women almost exclusively. And men who performed useful tasks like blacksmithing or sculpting architectural details, while respected to a degree, were not viewed as sharing the character traits of artists: intense, sometimes eccentric, potentially genius. Meanwhile, the skill with which a woman—or more accurately a girl—could sew became tied to her virtue. A young woman's ability to create items for her dowry or hope chest signaled her ability to one day become a good and pure wife. This philosophy put the final nail in the coffin of embroidery ever being seen as a "true" art form. How could women, stitching by candlelight, uneducated in the ways of philosophy, politics, war—and if wealthy kept from any kind of paid labor—be creating anything as grand and important as art?

Spoiler alert: they most certainly were. But very few, if any, thought so at the time. Thanks to twentieth century feminist thinker and civil rights activist Audre Lorde and Carol Hanisch's 1969 essay, "The Personal Is Political" we now have the language to reflect back, and even to see a possibly subversive nature to some of the stitching that was happening then. And I, for one, say hallelujah to this. We'll return to this idea of the personal being political later, but for now let's continue in our speedy history of art and craft in the Western world.

Alongside the Victorian era, toward the end of the eighteenth century, the Industrial Revolution had begun. In a flurry of innovation, machines began to make many of the things that earlier people could only make with their hands—clothes, books, furniture, and many other domestic items. Goods were made more easily and much more cost effectively.

Advances in art materials also occurred—artists could buy tubes of pre-made paint, making it easier for them to go outside. This also gave them stable colors that cost less. No more waiting for a shipment of the lapis that cost more than gold to create the ultramarine blue. No more grinding that lapis by hand and mulling it into a consistency with a binder in the studio to create paint. Hello, Impressionism! Huge leaps occurred in the way artists both thought about their work and made their work. Art was also no longer dependent on the church. More artists began to make work about things that interested them—not just stories or portraits—things that they philosophized about. Work that was increasingly beautiful for beauty's sake.

With every huge leap in technology comes a reaction—often a counter or backlash. The British designer William Morris gathered together a bunch of likeminded people who were fed up with what they saw as the unimaginative unoriginality of mass manufactured goods. In an attempt to return beauty and artistry to books, jewelry, furniture, wallpaper, metalwork, textiles, and other useful items, Morris founded Morris and Company and spawned what came to be known as the Arts and Crafts Movement. (Oh look—it's our two favorite words *together*!)

Known for flourishing patterns that often featured natural motifs of flora and fauna, and influenced by Medieval Gothic forms, Morris'

But Where Are You From From? Hopi, 2022, watercolor, embroidery, metallic paper, pins on yupo paper, 14 x 11 inches

From From Japan, 2022, watercolor, embroidery/thread, pins on Yupo paper 35 x 23 inches

aesthetic spread far and wide. Images were first meticulously sketched—with painters generating designs that are still recognizable today—the motifs were then translated by skilled tradespeople onto an array of practical goods for use in the home. By the 1880s, Morris had inspired the next generation to reinvigorate the guild system and declare that there was no meaningful difference between the fine and decorative arts.

The philosophies of these Englishmen spread to compatriots in America where the Arts and Crafts movement flourished into the 1920s. It also spread across Europe adopting the name Art Nouveau. While the English subscribers to the movement felt that everything should be handmade, the US counterparts were more amenable to manufactured goods that had the look and feel of hand-crafted items. With the rising costs of maintaining collaborative work areas, and the ascension of manufacturing, World War I helped usher in the demise of the movement. However, its tenents remain solidly believed in by many of today's makers.

The English were not alone in their desire to dismantle barriers between art and craft. The Bauhaus movement in Germany grew out of an art school operating from 1919 to 1933. Bauhaus practitioners labored to find a marriage between mass production and artistic vision. Unlike the swirly, organic forms of the Arts and Crafts movement, Bauhaus leaned into simple geometric shapes. It also pushed further into architecture. Bauhaus is seen as the beginning of Modernist ideas. What we think of now as "contemporary" aesthetics—with clean lines, abstraction—began with the Bauhaus. The movement also attempted to implement technology into the conversation, and changed how design and art were taught to up-and-coming creatives.

It's impossible to overstate how the Industrial Revolution flipped ideas surrounding the handmade on their head. Prior to the eighteenth Century, *everything* was hand made. There were no factories. There were tools and innovation (looms, stoves), but no mass creation. No one was making cakes or clothes or chairs on a grand scale. Rich people could afford to have other people make things for them. Poor people made the things they needed for themselves.

After the Industrial Revolution: anyone who could afford to just bought what they needed. We're so used to this now that it's hard to understand how radical a change it was at the time. There was also *status* in owning manufactured goods—imagine the delight in owning lace that *didn't* take five thousand hours and ten pairs of hands to make (especially if that time was your own). There was a whole economy of scale, with goods made inexpensive enough for the masses to purchase. And status got complicated quickly. Sometimes people were seen as poor and less-than if they had to make their own things. But in some instances the things that were handmade were now of superior value because of the time and effort and skill involved in their increasingly rare bespoke creations.

Today, it feels like we have reached peak tension in this conversation. We can purchase a $5 scarf that is a knock-off of a famous fashion house (or perhaps it is even designed by them) at a big box store. We can buy the mid- or high-priced $100 scarf from that fashion house directly. Or we can buy a scarf made by a fellow human with their hands—we can choose from a range of quality of yarns for whatever price that human can command on Etsy or their own website. It's not outrageous to see a custom, hand-knit scarf made from wool sustainably sheared from ethically-raised sheep, dyed the perfect shade you desire, in a single-source vat of natural dye, by someone named Sheena in Australia, for $500.

Is Sheena's scarf craft? Is it art? Is it art because we *value* it more? If it wasn't $500, would we relegate it back to craft? Or is it art because there is only one—and no one can quite make it the way Sheena does? Is that last fact even of importance? I would argue yes. Especially as we sit on the precipice of AI that can generate imagery on demand of anything at all without the need for a single human to draw, paint, or edit said imagery.

Of course, we know the debate between art and craft didn't die a peaceful death once Bauhaus exited stage right. And, anyway, Bauhaus never exited—for one thing it is still taught and admired—for another, it happened alongside Dada-ism, which lead to Modernism, which lead to Minimalism and Pop Art, and so on and so on. What also hasn't died is the debate between what constitutes fine art materials and craft materials.

While people inside the contemporary art and craft world (worlds?) don't seem to have quite as rigid a categorizations of materials front of mind these days, just for kicks let's try to acknowledge what it seems to be, at least to John Q. Public. At any rate, this is what I've seen after decades in the art world—working in galleries, as a working artist, teaching, and hanging around the art neighborhood. With the caveat—which I think you know by now—that I don't prescribe to this categorization myself at all.

Chroma Doilies, 2015, crochet doilies, threadballs and glasshead pins
76 x 28 x 14 inches, installed at Gallery CA, Baltimore MD

The Unspoken Hierarchy of Art Materials

Painting—oil painting in particular—seems to always be near the top of the art heap. Acrylic paint is a close second, but it still has ties to house paint—and while in the case of Jackson Pollock that was an artistic statement for many it's not "fine" enough (see how this is still perpetually confusing?). Watercolor and gouache are seen to oscillate between those who make art, and those who are hobbyists.

Drawing (unless it's a schematic of a subsequent art piece, or unless it's not actually drawing but in fact illustration) is definitely art.

Photography is art unless it's commercial—like for postcards or portraits for a website. Fashion photography skirts a line—sometimes it's high art, sometimes it's low. Single one-of-a-kind photos are more valuable than prints that are in multiples.

Printmaking—same. Overall, things on paper are usually valued less than things on canvas, walls, or wood. Even paintings on paper are of less value. Acceptable drawing materials do not usually include child's crayons, but context is key.

Sculpture —if it's metal and made in a foundry or involves certain subjects, yes art. Carving marble—yes art (but who does that anymore?). Wood—depends, if it's not functional, more likely. Memorial sculpture, or a statue of someone or something in a public place is not *as* fine art as a work that may depict a famous person or place but *isn't* commissioned by the state or said person.

Installations and video or new media—for *sure* are art perhaps especially if people can't understand them.

Ceramics, textiles/fiber, paper arts, glass, small metals/jewelry—all live in a region of can-be-art-but-can-also-just-be-craft.

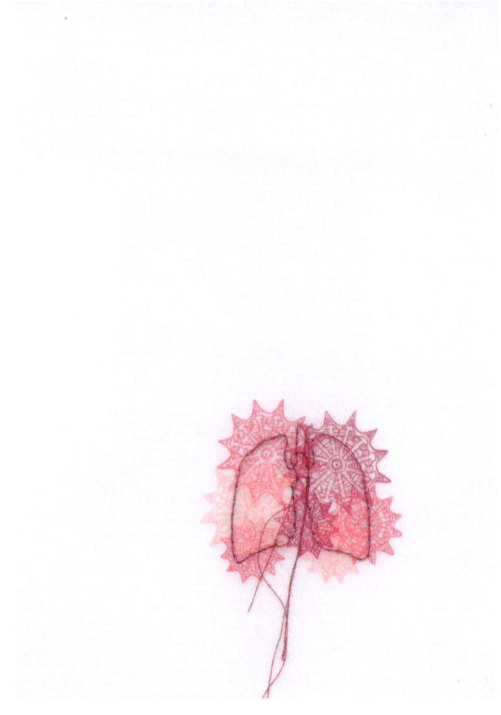

Doily Body : lungs, 2006, colored pencil and embroidery on duralar, 12 x 9 inches

Contemporary Craft

This is the perfect segue to a movement that has flourished during my own time in the arts: contemporary craft. Remember what I said I tell my students about materials lending themselves to preconceived notions, about pasta and dried-goods art? We've come back around to that.

If objects made using ceramic, textiles/fiber, glass, or small metals are functional and useful, they are often considered crafts. In fact, this alignment in our minds of utility and craft is so strong, that even if something we'd otherwise consider artwork is made for the specific utilitarian purpose of being sold to a consumer, it is often recategorized as a craft. This is even true with painting and photography. People perceive the painter or photographer selling tourist prints at a craft fair to not be a fine artist, regardless of the quality of their work. This is, of course, inherently contradictory as the fine art we see in galleries and museums is also bought and sold (often for grand fortunes), but the commerce side of the art world is continually shrouded in mystery. It's the quiet part we try not to say out loud. Because fine art is "good for us." It makes us think or weep; it changes our hearts and minds; it exposes us to culture. We like to believe it sort of lives outside of the boundaries of consumerism. We imagine it is "pure." If there aren't five of the exact same paintings marketed to you for the purpose of decorating your house—then it's art. If you are on your one hundredth painting of the same black cat that you sell at the farmer's market on weekends to pay your rent—it's probably craft.

In the 1970s, as feminism exploded across both academia and households around the world, female artists began to adopt the lexicon of the movement in their work. "The personal is political" meant that things relegated to a feminine sphere were inherently infused with politics. Doing the dishes, taking care of kids, and a person's ability to choose *not* to do any of these assigned tasks and roles became of importance. By extension, tasks often done by women for the home—sewing, knitting, weaving, embroidering—became the materials used to make art about those restraints. Or art about just being a woman. Or subversive art. Using these low-brow, non-art materials for high-brow art became way more interesting. So did using glass, or small metals, or ceramics, or any materials usually pushed out of the "important" (male) art arena. Shelia Hicks, Eve Hesse, and Ruth Asawa (to name just a very few) all propelled these ideas into the art-o-sphere and ensured that they were taken seriously. (If you want to learn more about this idea, check out Rosalika Parker's academic work *The Subversive Stitch*.)

But the ideas of education (do you need an MFA to make important art?) and use (thrown pottery mugs are not the same as thrown pottery sculptures) still asserted their dominance. And no matter the strides feminist art had made, craft still seemed like a stepchild. Sure, punk helped usher in a DIY aesthetic and attitude—a make-it-yourself and make-it-a-statement vibe that was easily co-opted into fine art—but there was still often a feeling of looking down on certain types of materials and how people used them.

This seemed amplified in 2003 when the California College of Arts and Crafts (CCAC)—one of the oldest private art institutions and a staple in my own hometown of Oakland, California—decided to drop that last C and become the California College of Art (CCA). CCAC had been a hub of huge leaps in ceramics. It even had a renowned textile department, a thing very few art schools had—a dedicated course of study for textiles that, at least on paper, had the same clout as any dedicated course of study for painting or video art.

I remember the raw rage that many people felt in learning that craft was no longer of importance to CCA. A new San Francisco campus was also unveiled. And the Oakland campus, housed in a historic Victorian home alongside decades-old various studios and facilities—became effectively the back-burner campus. (And at this moment is waiting to be sold off and not in use by the college at all). The real, new, and important art was being made in San Francisco, in a new and important building which no longer would be tarnished with the historical context of craft. Craft was a relic. Contemporary making didn't need to be concerned with craft.

People also were overjoyed! Of course, craft—in the sense of how to actually make things, how to use tools, what kind of formal choices to make—was still important, but why muddy the waters of grand art with the commerciality of craft? Dropping that C felt liberating to these people. They could now just get down to the core of what they were all here to do.

To me, it seemed odd that this was happening at around the exact time that a resurgence in interest in craft materials and crafting was bubbling under the surface of the art world. I graduated with my MFA in 2003 showing large scale embroideries and a blanket made out of crocheted wire that spoke in my grandmother's voice. I then went on to make drawings of doilies—the crocheted bits that sat on the backs of sofas and under vases, the kind of thing that grandmas and old-fashioned people made, or that young people re-purposed with tongues firmly planted in their cheeks. I next turned to felt, textiles, and various traditional techniques to explore all kinds of concepts—warfare, disease, and my own cultural identity as a bi-racial woman.

I wasn't alone. Soon the doily exploded across the design world. More and more artists began using thread and embroidery in their work. In 2009 *Handmade Nation*—a documentary about the rise of DIY, art, and craft—made its debut and solidified that this was a cultural phenomenon; the discussion about art and craft was happening everywhere by a lot of makers; and it wasn't going away.

At this very moment, a quarter of the way into the twenty-first century, we can't get away from artists and makers presenting embroidery, marbling, block printing, spoon carving and so many other crafts in their online performances on social media. These people call themselves artists. They work both within and outside of the traditional art world. They take themselves seriously. But often they still do not know if they are making art or craft and people will still relegate their wares into those categories.

Outside the West

This seems like a good moment to pause for a second and move away from our Western world discussion. We in the West are very interested in the philosophy, the scope, the representation, the theory, and the meaning behind art and subsequently craft. The Eastern world seemingly sees a much less adversarial and more symbiotic relationship between the two. In my experience, Eastern artists and craftspeople are given practically equal reverence. The conversation is more about skill. It is also about dedication—that all art and craft take time and mastery. If you are dedicated and serious enough, then you are seen as worthy.

I watched an interview with an apprentice miso fermenter. The miso had to sit in vats that were surrounded and weighted by huge rocks for many years. The rocks were used over and over and chosen and placed very carefully. The miso rock master was teaching his apprentice how to pick and stack the boulders so that they would form pleasing pyramids. The pyramids not only had to distribute the weight evenly to make the best possible miso, but they had to look good too. The apprentice had been doing this alongside his teacher for three years, but he humbly explained he wasn't good enough yet. That there was a true art to stacking these boulders. He hoped in a few more years he would be able to perhaps attempt to make a pyramid without anyone checking his work. Then he might be considered generally competent and proficient at this task.

This whole premise—of making something utilitarian that has a component of aesthetic proficiency as well—is something we don't discuss much in the Western world. These concepts—that the useful pyramid is *not as good* if it doesn't also please the eye and it can take *years* to get to a point of barely being good at making something—are not relatable to most of the students I teach. Maybe there used to be more of an apprenticeship model followed for some arts/crafts, but it seems to have left the building. If you'll allow me to generalize and stereotype for a moment: it feels like Western makers are more interested in prioritizing being avant-garde and unique, and pursuing the individuality of what they are making. Sure, someone taught them how to do something originally, but it's *their* genius or mojo that moves what they are making into importance.

There are other cultural narratives that feed into this as well. For one thing, we often prescribe to a "fake it until you make it" doctrine, actively encouraging people to keep doing things when they don't know what they're doing. And in contemporary art specifically there has been a huge shift toward embracing the premise that education and mastery of tools and materials may actually sometimes even be bad. There's an almost magical story of the untrained artist—that if someone is genuinely inspired, a mysterious embodiment occurs and true art just pours out of them. Nothing can stop it.

Perhaps we can attribute some of the variance in the Eastern approach to a Buddhist concept of

Tsuri /fishing/, 2024, Gelli monoprints on paper, 12 x 9 inches each 72 x 72 inches this configuration, installed at Walter Maciel Gallery, Los Angeles, CA

being in the moment. The art or craft is thus not a symbol of the world, but a revelation of the artist in that precise moment in time. Everything made can thus be a reflection of beauty or any other feeling or perception. It is fleeting and never precisely repeatable. The gesture, the thoughts, the action, the objects, the arrangement, the state of mind—all are of equal importance. So is the person who presents it. The tools used to make it. Nothing stands singularly alone—everything relates to the larger world. Spontaneity is considered as well as skill. There is a skill in being able to enter into a spontaneous space. And there is a deep understanding that even if superficially looking the same, anything that is made by a person is impossibly personal and unrepeatable. The first circle painted with sumi ink cannot possibly be the same as the five-hundredth one. The hand will tire. The ink will flow differently. Your wrist will shift.

The respect that is given to artisans in the East also feels different. In the West, artists are often not taken seriously unless their work sells. And, even then, the where and how much it sells for matters. In the East, too, there are of course hierarchical notions of importance and seriousness, but there is also a respect for anyone who does their job well. An underlying understanding that a person who makes the best croissant is as interesting and important as a person who makes the best bird drawing. In the West this importance often runs parallel or in conjunction with fame.

Intent and Choices

How seriously we take people might bring us around, if by a somewhat winding path, to something else we haven't talked about yet. Something that is, in fact, one of the most commonly and strongly held beliefs by Western folks entering into this art and craft discourse; and that is the concept of intent. In conversation, many artists will declare it's the *intent* that matters—the artist's own concept, their research. It's art once I, the maker, say it is. And it's hard to argue against this.

Ever since Marcel Duchamp effectively waved his magic art wand by turning a urinal upside down, signing it (with a fake name), and putting it on a pedestal, the idea that *anything* can be art was born. And since then, artists have indeed made art out of everything—bodily fluids, trash, army-issued blankets, shoes—you get the idea. If you have a concept and make the declaration, it's art.

I've also heard artists say that craft is what is used to *make* the art. So, an artist can absorb the tenets of craft, but then *elevate* those crafts into art. Kind of like waving a magic art wand again.

Some have said that art is made when we are seeking, questioning. That it should be an expansive and not retractive ideology. These folks argue that it's not the labeling of art or craft that matters, that instead anything can be either/or to anyone because both creator and viewer bring their own life and experience to the table.

Others may argue that craft, on the other hand, is simply following a pattern. Making something useful, for consumption. Less valuable—even if it costs *a lot* more than a similar manufactured item from a store.

Then there are those who think it's all the same. The person who makes a blanket for a bed is the same as a person who makes a blanket that hangs on a museum wall. The Gees Bend quilts were meant to be utilitarian—the makers never said they were making art or wanted to make art—but they *are* art because they are sublime, beautiful, innovative. In this scenario it isn't just the artist who can wave the art wand, but a curator, a society, an observer.

I always return to a conversation I had with my grandmother one time when I was in the thick of thinking about art and craft. She was a huge supporter of anything I did, including pursuing art. She was fascinated by what made good art, bad art, and by why I was even thinking about art and craft in general and particularly within my own work. Any time we'd go

Amime Net Knots, 2023 (525 in configuration) detail, hand dyed and tied rope, 132 x 287 inches installed at San Luis Obispo Museum of Art, CA, photo credit: Stephen Heraldo

to a museum or even a restaurant, she would ask me what I thought about what was on the wall. And I would give her an honest assessment. And then she'd probe me. At an Asian restaurant she asked why I scoffed at the Pier One-style prints of circles. I said they felt hollow and to look at Enso masters or even Richard Serra's circle drawings to see if she felt a difference. She did.

So, one day I asked her if she ever felt like she was an artist or that she had missed a calling. She was incredibly adept at making things with her hands. She knitted; she crocheted; she could execute with precision the very challenging hardanger embroidery (where you count and snip threads generating holes and ensuring those holes are surround stitched). She immediately responded, "Oh no, I am definitely not an artist. And even if I was properly trained, I don't think I have what it takes." I pushed back, "But Grammy, you are so good with your hands. And you make beautiful, artful things."

She insisted that she wasn't creative because she mostly followed patterns. I insisted that she made all of the same choices I did with artwork. She chose colors, always different than those pictured. She chose yarn and thread. She often re-imagined patterns making adjustments or winging it and changing the collars, or lengths, or fit, or something in the design. Adding a flower here or a button there. I said perhaps if she just copied someone's designs, or didn't spend so much time thinking about what she was making, then I might agree that perhaps there was less of an artistic approach to her way of making things. But that, at the very least, I totally saw her as a creative thinker and maker. She smiled and seemed to like that.

And this is where I will leave you, dear whatever-you'd-like-to-label-yourself. We are back where we began. Perhaps with no huge discovery or breakthrough in understanding. Perhaps you, like me, will now commence to think about this over and over. Your mind might change. You might come to a new and more secure conclusion. I know that every time I asked one of the artists in this book what they thought about art and craft I digested their thoughtful responses and nodded my head. I know that each of them carefully and artfully crafted the projects you see in these pages. Some of them leaned into art history references, or their art school background, or adopted techniques and materials that straddle the very divide I feel I have been unable to fully name, describe, or reconcile for you here (though I have certainly given it my best shot!).

I think in the end my sincere hope is that you are inspired to make something from this book because it speaks to you. Because I know from experience, and from witnessing it in my classrooms and workshops, what happens when people make things with their own hands. It's always a good thing. Even when it's a struggle, the end result is worth any difficulty. The wonder, the empathy, the sense of accomplishment, the creativity, the imagination, the toil—it all ends up in the thing we make. What we make tells a story. And we humans are wired to tell and hear these stories. It's how we are connected. It's how we find meaning. It's how we are most ourselves.

COLOR

by Lisa Solomon

Like many children, I grew up drawing and painting rainbows. Truth be told, perhaps I was a little more obsessed than most. I tended to make full arch rainbows. In bright blue skies. With puffy white clouds on either end. Then I expanded my repertoire to include cats, sitting on hearts, with rainbows above their heads. Rainbows were placed on objects I drew—on figures' t-shirts, on book covers, surrounding tableware. You get the idea. And then one day they stopped showing up in my drawings. I can't exactly pinpoint when, but they were prominent no more.

In grad school when I was getting my MFA in the early 2000s, a couple of hoity-toity artists visited my studio to talk to me about my work. I started by giving them a little spiel about what I was thinking and why I was doing the work they were looking at. They cut me off and asked, "what did you used to draw all the time when you were a kid?" A bit taken aback I told them what I remembered more than anything was cats sitting on hearts with rainbows over their heads. They nodded and said, "You should return to that."

At the time I giggled. That's kind of preposterous. Cats sitting on hearts? But a part of me thought, "hmm, maybe that's not so silly?" With all the talk of conceptualism and Art with a capital A, and a capital M for Meaning—could I justify cute Hello Kitty-inspired cats with rainbows floating above them? Wouldn't I just be entering into a Lisa Frank lexicon of absolute absurd non seriousness? At the time I was also grappling with the idea that art could and should be *about* anything. The concept that the material itself, or a simple color, could in fact be the content was increasingly important to me. That capital M now stood for two things: Meaning and Material.

This was also around the time I started a blog. Suddenly, the internet cracked wide open and became a filter—a way to find like-minded folks around the world who shared the same likes and dislikes. It was pretty clear that those of us posting similar photographs—of corners of our homes, our collections, our artistic spottings, and our own work—(first on Flickr, then on our own blogs, then on Pinterest) were in this together.

In those years, the early aughts, someone's post of a bookshelf arranged by color exploded across the net. People seemed to either love or hate it. On one side, it was hailed as both beautiful and useful. On the other it was detracted as a complete waste of time—and liking it meant that you weren't serious about reading.

As with the whole art/craft debate I myself could easily straddle this divide. Part of me was charmed by the rainbow bookshelf. Things in Red-Orange-Yellow-Green-Blue-Indigo-Violet order just make sense to the human brain. But part of me was wondering if I would personally ever bother to take the time to complete such a task. When it came to making art, I could easily justify the time needed to complete a project—but did I want to endeavor to make my home that aesthetic? (To this day, as much time as I've spent putting things in rainbow order, my books are not, nor have they ever been, organized by ROYGBIV.)

Why do we naturally smile when we see a rainbow in the sky? Or when we tilt a prism and the sun casts tiny rainbows across a room? If you want to wax philosophical, perhaps it's simply our inherent response to the wonder of nature. Rainbows seem magical. We can understand the scientific principles behind them—light refracting off water or a prism—but it still seems like a gift. Even when I was in Hawaii, where I could spy more than one rainbow a day, each sighting sparked a moment of pure joy and wonder.

I think as humans we are wired to seek out these kinds of experiences. Maybe because it makes us feel more alive. Maybe because it forces us to look past the everydayness of our lives that can become mundane and humdrum. Maybe because a rainbow reminds us of our humanity—that, like them, we need light and water and that we too are filled with a bit of color and magic. Or maybe because in the moment we spot a rainbow we realize that there is a whole universe that surrounds us and, like us, it too can create beauty if the conditions are just so.

As I moved through my own relationship to color and reading every treatise I could find on it—learning about pigments and how our brains process them—I kept reflecting back to that studio visit. Should I just take the plunge and create more rainbows in my work? What would that look like? What would it mean? And then fate stepped in to make rainbows a much larger part of my life.

Christine Buckton Tillman and I met on Flickr. We had a few mutual art pals. We admired each other's work. A lot. For me it was *more* than the typical oh-I-really-like-and-respect-this-and-want-something-of-yours-in-my-home-to-look-at-on-a-daily-basis. It was the pull of familiarity. We both had similar visual vocabularies. An interest in materials—we both questioned why some were considered more "important" and "art-worthy" than others. And we both loved and gravitated to color. Striking color combinations. Things in rainbows or rainbow adjacent—that is, in the right order, but not quite the typical rainbow color: like a tangerine instead of an orange, a pinkish rose instead of bright red.

We talked for years about joining forces, collaborating on something large in scale. And in 2015 we got our chance. We were offered a space in Baltimore (Christine's home town) to do whatever our hearts' desired. The debate and research on what to do began in earnest. Since color and color theory and the exploration of often overlooked/mundane objects in our everyday worlds were themes in both our work, we pushed in that direction. In the end we worked on a series of drawings together—each starting them and sending them to the other to finish. And we decided that we also wanted to attempt a crowd-sourced installation of objects sent to us from all over the world. We weren't sure how many people would participate (turned out lots!). All we asked was for people to send us objects, roughly no larger than a person's palm, that were plastic or paper, and mostly one color. We wanted the "detritus" of our lives—the plastic bread ties, broken or no longer wanted toys, small balls of yarn, crayons, binder clips, and on and on. We had a loose plan of arranging the objects in chromatic order, but it was a very loose plan because who knew what we'd get and what could happen.

drawing from my childhood

It's always slightly daunting and very exciting to arrive in a clean space with a slim semblance of a plan. But we quickly got going, dumping the thousands of objects that we had presorted into general color schemes onto the concrete floor. Christine and I set to work. ABK was our anthem (ABK stands for Always Be Knolling—this refers to laying things flat and arranging them in neat parallel lines or ninety degree angles). We discovered that we had endless choices to make. Where would red be? Left, right, top, bottom? How would we consider value? In long stripes? In groupings from a direction? Where would pink go? With the reds or with the purples? What about black, white, brown, metallics? Some browns lent themselves to oranges or dark yellow, but other browns not so much. It was interesting and eye opening to not have to make all of these decisions by myself. As a team we could bounce ideas off of one another and argue a point—but mostly we just quickly concurred. Here I was with someone who cared as much as me about these subtleties. It felt like a mini miracle that I wasn't alone in my color obsessiveness.

We ended up working from right to left, with darker values at the top, lighter-closer-to-white values toward the bottom. Thus, we placed dark red objects in the upper right corner, moving into pink, then orange, yellow, lime, green, all the blues, slivers of purple, black, gray, and white. Silvers, golds, and browns/neutrals got their own area (this ended up being a small wall to the left of the large expanse everything else went on). We also decided to create a more organic shape. Something that didn't have a sharp top or bottom line.

I can attest that there is an art to making a gradient. An ombre. Maybe it's actually less of an art and more of a skill. We quickly realized that we loved and desperately needed what we now deem "transitional objects." These are things that have maybe seven colors on them but that we can place in a spot where we need to leap from one tone to another—the green bit blends in with the green area where it's living, and the orange bit relates to the orange objects several feet away.

Our eyes blend the things together and say: *yes*, this makes sense to me. Maybe our transitional object had just two colors. A perfect blend of yellow and orange that we can place in a space that helps build the bridge between the yellow and orange objects.

I can also attest that there is a lot of random color in our lives. That we usually end up with way more blue objects than any other color. And that we always have the fewest purple objects. This lines up with my very unscientific theory: you can divide a room by purple. I have put this into practice and you can too! First ask any group of people in a room who likes purple and who doesn't. People will have definite opinions. Some *very* definite. You can then further divide the purple-liking people into those who like red purples and those who like blue purples. It's very rare to have someone who will be amenable to all the purples all the time. But very few arguments will ever be had over green.

Once we had all our objects arranged on the gray floor—fiddling with a placement here and a transitional object there—we transferred the items (with *a lot* of amazing volunteer help) to the white wall, where once again the whole thing transformed. The colors popped off the white background. The undulation of ochre to lemon to lime to forest green became more than just the sum of all these parts. It became a visually satisfying, dare I say, *phenomenon*. One where stepping back gave one the perception of a finely-tuned rainbow delight.

And as one got closer it became the most complicated "I Spy" game ever—watching people exclaim, "Oh a LaCroix!" "A water gun!" "Storm troopers!" We included some items that had

Lisa Solomon + Christine Buckton Tillman, *Chroma*, 2015, donated objects, dimensions variable this configuration 144 x 316 inches installed at Gallery CA, Baltimore, MD photo credit: Stewart Watson

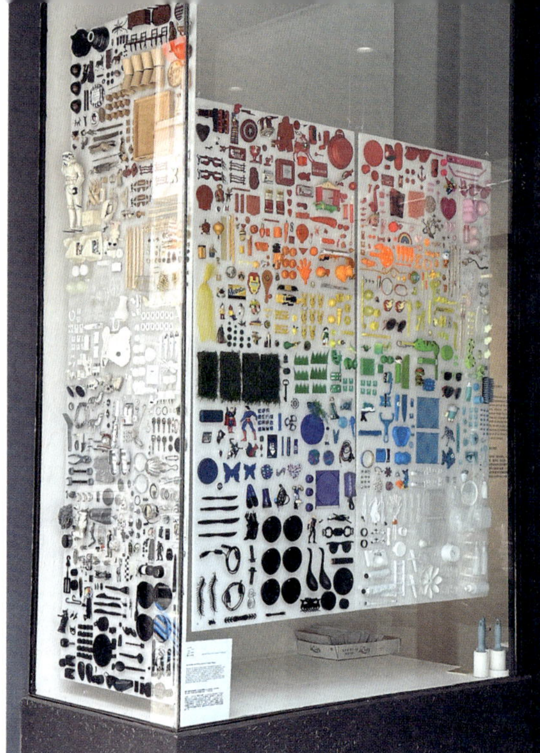

Lisa Solomon + Christine Buckton Tillman, *Chroma - SF Chinatown*, 2023, donated objects on plexiglass, 96 x 30 and 72 x 64 inches, installed at Edge on the Square, San Francisco, CA

personal value—like my kiddo's ballet slippers. The act of collecting, sorting, and arranging—pulling all the like colors together—added so much wonder and beauty and glee. Who knew that twelve turquoise bread ties with small dark blue dates stamped onto them would create the most pleasing grid when tucked between fake sushi grass and a silicone spatula? Well, now we do and we were hooked.

We have taken the Chroma show on the road. We've made smaller permanent pieces for homes; a more public permanent piece in an apartment building on the Wharf in Washington, DC; and two exhibitions in San Francisco—one at Rare Device Gallery and another in the windows of a gallery space in Chinatown. And, most recently, Chroma has traveled to our dream locale—Japan (because Japan does make some of the cutest plastic drink tops known to humans). Each time we've done something slightly different. Each time we walk away with new ideas and possibilities. Each time we still feel like we want to do it again. Each time I feel like I am reinforcing some of my opinions about color and color theory, and making new ones or overlaying new concepts on top of the old. Fantastically each time we get faster at it too. It's the Ten Thousand Hour Rule in action.

All of which is to say: I no longer think working in or with rainbows is a cop-out or not serious enough. I continually arrange supplies in my studio by color. It actually really helps me focus and choose what color I want to use. And it looks f-ing cool. I have been asked to re-arrange many a friend's art supplies or other items this way too. I pretty much always oblige. Sometimes I do it slyly and covertly and in random places. A small move of a lipstick here or there to make the make-up display a tad more pleasing.

Basic human knowledge involves color. Why are we constantly asking each other—even tiny children—what is our favorite? Why does our favorite change now and again? Granted, some of us are more obsessed. We can talk forever about periwinkle. Whether, in our heads, it leans more blue or more lavender, more aqua or more violet—discuss. No one is ever wrong about their own personal color sense. You can only have different opinions from other people. In that way color is both an incredibly intimate thing, and a way to help us navigate the world together (hand me my orange socks please).

Using color as a parameter is a perfect framework. When I'm stuck creatively, I'll limit myself to using just one or two colors. Stretching the possibilities in the color—making a red move from carmine to vermillion and swoop to pink—is always a worthwhile task. I'm continually interested in seeing the same thing in different colors—from clothing to dishware—to see how color alone can change our perceptions of a particular item. Given a choice between a white and an avocado-colored bowl, I'll contemplate the contents and my mood and choose accordingly.

The Colors in This Book

In this book, we present twenty projects for you to try. Twenty well-developed, thought-provoking, occasionally amusing and fun, sometimes useful, and dare I say beautiful, items for you to make. We assigned each maker a color for them to work with. It was quite delightful to hear the response from these incredible makers to their colors. Some were immediately excited as their color fit their work and personal palette perfectly. Some asked if they could include other colors and how much of them. Some wanted to verify precisely what we meant by "lime green." Thankfully no one groaned.

In thinking of the hues, we thought very broadly—although we did subcategorize into lights and darks. We included black, white, and gray, as of course we should. We wanted each artist to choose *their own* red or yellow. We didn't include brown, not because there aren't moments where we love brown, but because when we made a list of colors, it seemed potentially challenging to ask someone to make something in brown that would fit in with this list of colors, unless we suggested about four different shades of brown, and that seemed like too much for a book that is essentially a rainbow. We could be right, or very very wrong about that. And that is where we leave it to you to decide. Maybe you want to make everything in this book in brown. Or in every color. Multiple tea towels. Multiple basket bowls. Maybe you want to make them exactly as you see them. Or make something for a friend in their current favorite color. The only thing placing any limits on this is you.

WHY THESE FOLKS NOW?

by Lisa Solomon

What is it that brought together this particular collection of brilliant artists and makers?

The short answer is that these are all people whose work I have known, loved, and respected for many years. The long answer has a number of parts. We wanted a cross section of mediums—not just textiles but food, flowers, paper. We wanted people who see themselves as Artists with a capital A, Crafters with a capital C, and people who purposefully straddle that divide. We were also invested in making sure to include folks from various regions and cultural backgrounds, and at different points in their making journeys. Ultimately, though, I felt like everyone had to pass the would-I-speak-with-them-about-the-grand-ideas-of-art-and-craft test. All of these people are invested. They are professional. They care deeply about what they make and why they make it. I have, in fact, had the what is the difference/is there a difference between art and craft conversation with many of the contributors. Some of them more than once. These conversations are ones that helped me form, or solidified, my own responses to ideas surrounding art and craft.

I love community and collaboration, but so much of the act of creativity exists inside of us. We labor alone. Even when we work in a group, we spend some portion of time, effort, and research alone. Even if we have teams of folks to bounce ideas off of, at some point to be creative is to find that space inside one's self where that spark of magic happens. Whenever I get to nerd out with another maker over a type of watercolor, a specific glue, or a hack that has worked in my studio, I feel it is a gift.

This book feels like bringing a colorful collection of friends and flavors together for a joyous potluck. If we weren't already friends, we are now. I hope that spirit of community and collaboration inspires you as you flip through this book. Make the things that jump out at you. Do not feel obligated to make them exactly as you see them. Change their colors to ones you love. Experiment until you find your color palette. Allow that palette to change. Get your hands dirty. Open your mind. Explore the art, craft, and color that surrounds your daily life. Most of all, have fun.

PART TWO

The Projects

opera rose
indigo
vermillion
indigo
34
No. 40. Imperial Purple, is azure and
blue, with carmine red, about
parts of each.
41. Auricula Purple, is plum purple, with
indigo blue and much carmine red.
42. Plum Purple, the plum blue of Werner, is composed of Berlin blue, with
much carmine red, a very little brown,
and an almost imperceptible portion
of black. W.
43. Red Lilac Purple, is campanula
ple, with a considerable
44. Lavender Pur
Werner, is
and a little brow
45. Pale Bluish
mixed with a

PALE PINK: Collage

CREATED BY

Christine Buckton Tillman

"Since 2020 I've been making collages from the photos I take on my phone. The world is full of the best colors and shapes just waiting to be pinned down in a composition. I'm always seeing little paintings out in the world. I started getting prints made at my local drugstore so I could cut them up and make something new. I take my favorites and turn them into paintings. Making is totally magical. My studio work is profoundly craft influenced, I use and reference traditional craft techniques like embroidery, quilting, and ceramics. I find joy in all kinds of making."

The term collage comes from the French word *coller* which means to glue. The first evidence of collage comes from China circa 200 BCE. Our modern-day relationship with collage was born in the early twentieth century. Picasso, Braque, and the Cubists first began pasting rectangle shapes atop existing drawings. Their experiments travelled to Spain and Russia and then were picked up by the Dadaists. The Dada movement—and artist Hannah Hoch in particular—used all kinds of found detritus including photographs. The Surrealists loved using seemingly mismatched imagery to generate new meanings and narratives then took it to the next level. Artists have been incorporating collage techniques ever since.

Most people have the supplies for collage hanging around the house. Magazines, photographs (both family and found), ephemera (receipts, tickets), and paper of all kinds (scraps of colored paper be it origami paper, child's construction paper, wrapping paper, etc.), scissors or utility knives, glue or tape, and voila! Some artists include other household items or place their collages onto scrap wood, inside boxes, under glass, and otherwise make things more permanent or complex—but truly, gluing one piece of paper to another is all you really need.

Collage is exciting because the combinations of materials and meanings is endless. Barbara Kruger utilized collage techniques to create incredibly powerful political work that turned the language of advertising on its head. Other contemporary artists have expanded collage into three dimensions using embroidery or textiles for texture and larger objects to make things more sculptural (see husband and wife teams Robert Rauschenberg and Susan Weil, and Ed and Nancy Kienholz). You can explore exacting and finicky collage using tweezers and fine blades to cut out small papers, or make loose and free-wheeling collages as large as can be imagined.

MATERIALS

- Commercially printed photos, magazine spreads, or photo quality paper inkjet/laser prints (my commercial prints come from the drug store in 4-by-4- or 4-by-6-inch / 10 by 10 or 10 by 15 cm prints)
- X-ACTO knife
- Cutting mat
- Acrylic medium (your choice gloss or matte) or mod podge
- Brush
- Two pieces of scrap paper

INSTRUCTIONS

1. Gather photos to use. (A) You can plan this out. I do not. I work with big piles of photos and often make several collages at a time playing with my images and deciding which is best.

2. Cut out shapes from different pictures. I generally flip through my stack looking for a shape I want to isolate. (B) Then I cut it out. (C)

3. Arrange and re-arrange, trying new combinations until satisfied. (D) Color, composition, and unexpected juxtapositions drive my choices; sometimes I search for one missing element, like a background.

4. The final collage will be 4-by-4 inches / 10-by-10 cm. To help imagine what it will look like, I flip over extra photos or use extra paper to create a frame. (E)

5. When I am satisfied with my composition, I prepare to glue. It's generally easier to glue from the back to the front. I put the piece I am going to glue right side down on a piece of scrap paper. Using a brush and acrylic medium, I coat the back of the paper with acrylic medium. (F) The scrap piece of paper keeps my desk clean, and I'm able to extend the glue past the edge of the paper so it doesn't build up on the edges.

A
B
C
D
E
F

6 I place the glued piece onto the photo I have chosen as the base. (G) Put a second clean piece of scrap paper down on top and press to burnish. (H) This process ensures you have good contact, and picks up any extra adhesive that may have squished out. If you continue to glue more pieces on top, make sure the paper you burnish with doesn't have any wet glue that might deposit on your collage. Remove the burnish paper, and let the collage dry.

7 As a last step, I trim the collage. (I) Using a 4-inch (10 cm) square photo or paper as a guide, I cut any pieces that overhang. Trimming is optional, so if you prefer uneven edges, by all means you can leave them or plan for them.

Christine Buckton Tillman is the Visual Arts Chair at The Park School of Baltimore, Maryland. She has taught and advised high schoolers for over two decades. She has been a member of the Drawing Center Viewing Program, DC Art Bank Program, and Transformer Flat File. She received a Maryland State Arts Council Grant for her Works on Paper. She is a two-time finalist for the Trawick Prize and has had her work published through Urban Outfitters.

Christine has exhibited across the United States. She has had solo and two-person shows at Material in Memphis, Tennessee, School 33 Art Center, and the World Trade Center in Baltimore, Maryland. Christine has been included in group shows with Latela Curatorial, Flashpoint, Transformer, the Katzen Museum in Washington, DC, and Grizzly Grizzly in Philadelphia. She has worked collaboratively with Lisa Solomon since 2015 on their project Chroma where they collect and categorize objects by color. They have installed Chroma in Baltimore, San Francisco, and Japan. Learn more at www.christinebucktontillman.com and on Instagram at @christinebucktontillman.

CHA

HOT PINK: Paper Toothbrush

CREATED BY

Libby Black

"In my practice, I find profound meaning in the moments between larger works—the creative 'cool down' that follows intense periods of artistic production. The paper Chanel toothbrush emerged from such a moment, following a 2018 exhibition in Germany, utilizing the remnants of paper from more substantial sculptures.

This piece playfully juxtaposes the mundane necessity of dental hygiene with the allure of luxury branding. The bristles, deliberately sculpted to splay outward, mirror the wear pattern of my own toothbrush—a personal detail that grounds this luxury object in the reality of daily use. By recreating a disposable tool in the guise of high fashion, I explore the tension between utility and exclusivity, necessity and excess.

The work has evolved into an ongoing series, with various sizes and luxury brands, becoming a ritual of artistic decompression. These pieces serve as meditations on consumer culture, examining how branding can transform even the most basic implements of daily life into objects of desire. Through paper—a humble, ephemeral medium—I reconstruct symbols of opulence, questioning the seduction of luxury and its integration into our most intimate routines."

Paper is an omnipresent item in our lives. Even as we move ever towards the digital, paper is everywhere. Paper has been used in art and crafting for centuries, and not only as simply a flat substrate for drawing and painting upon. Origami is a familiar paper folding practice and one that has been done for centuries. Paper sculpture, however—which incorporates more than just folding—is a relatively new practice, gaining popularity in the twentieth century.

Paper sculpture can use the folding techniques of origami, as well as cutting and layering, quilling (which is rolling and shaping strips of paper), and even carving shapes with tools—all to get from flat sheets of paper to the creation of a three-dimensional piece. The type and color of your paper has a huge influence on the work. The use of materials like paint and glue is also critical, to expand the formal qualities of the paper.

Simple paper sculptures often recreate flowers or smaller objects, while more complex ones get grand in scale. Paper can be used to make realistic forms, or abstract ones. It is even possible to consider the layered corrugated cardboard furniture that Charles and Rae Eames created—which is now considered a pinnacle of Midcentury Modernist design—as part of this tradition. There is a lot of versatility!

MATERIALS

- Hot glue gun
- Hot glue sticks
- Scissors
- Pencil
- Strathmore 400 Series Bristol Board 22-by-30 inches (56 by 76 cm), 4 Ply, Vellum (you will not use this whole sheet of paper, you could make a dozen with one sheet, but it is the best paper)
- Golden (or similar) Acrylic paint
  - Medium Magenta
  - Titanium White
  - Mars Black
  - Iridescent Bright Gold (Fine)
- Brushes (I used Princeton, but other brushes are fine)
  - liner brush 10/0
  - round brush 6

INSTRUCTIONS

1 Draw out the handle and head of your toothbrush as one piece and cut it out. (A)

2 Trace three times and cut those out. You will now have four. (B)

3 Glue all four stacked on top of each other, one layer at a time.

4 Draw a rectangle (this will be part of the bristles) and cut it out. Trace five more and cut them out. (C)

5 Draw out a small triangle to go on the back of the brush handle and cut it out. (This is the pick part of the toothbrush.) Trace twice, cut them out, and you will now have three same-size triangle pick pieces. (D) Glue them stacked together.

6 In each rectangle, cut into the paper three-quarters of the way through to make the bristles. (Make sure you don't cut the bristles all the way through the rectangle.)

7 Put a row of hot glue on the toothbrush head and put one of the rows of bristles in the glue. (E) Repeat until you are done with all six rows of the bristles for the toothbrush head. (F)

8 Run a bead of glue at the back of the brush and put your triangle pick in the glue. (G)

9 Paint the handle and head dark pink with your round brush. (H)

10 When the handle is dry, paint the bristles white. (I)

11 Do a second coat of dark pink on the handle and head of the toothbrush.

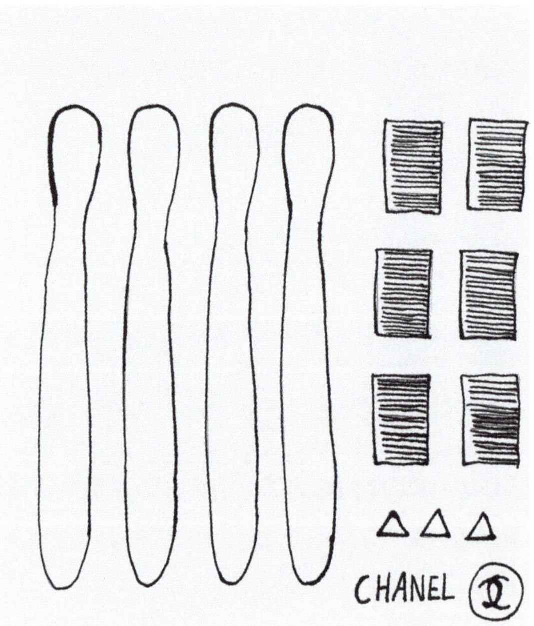

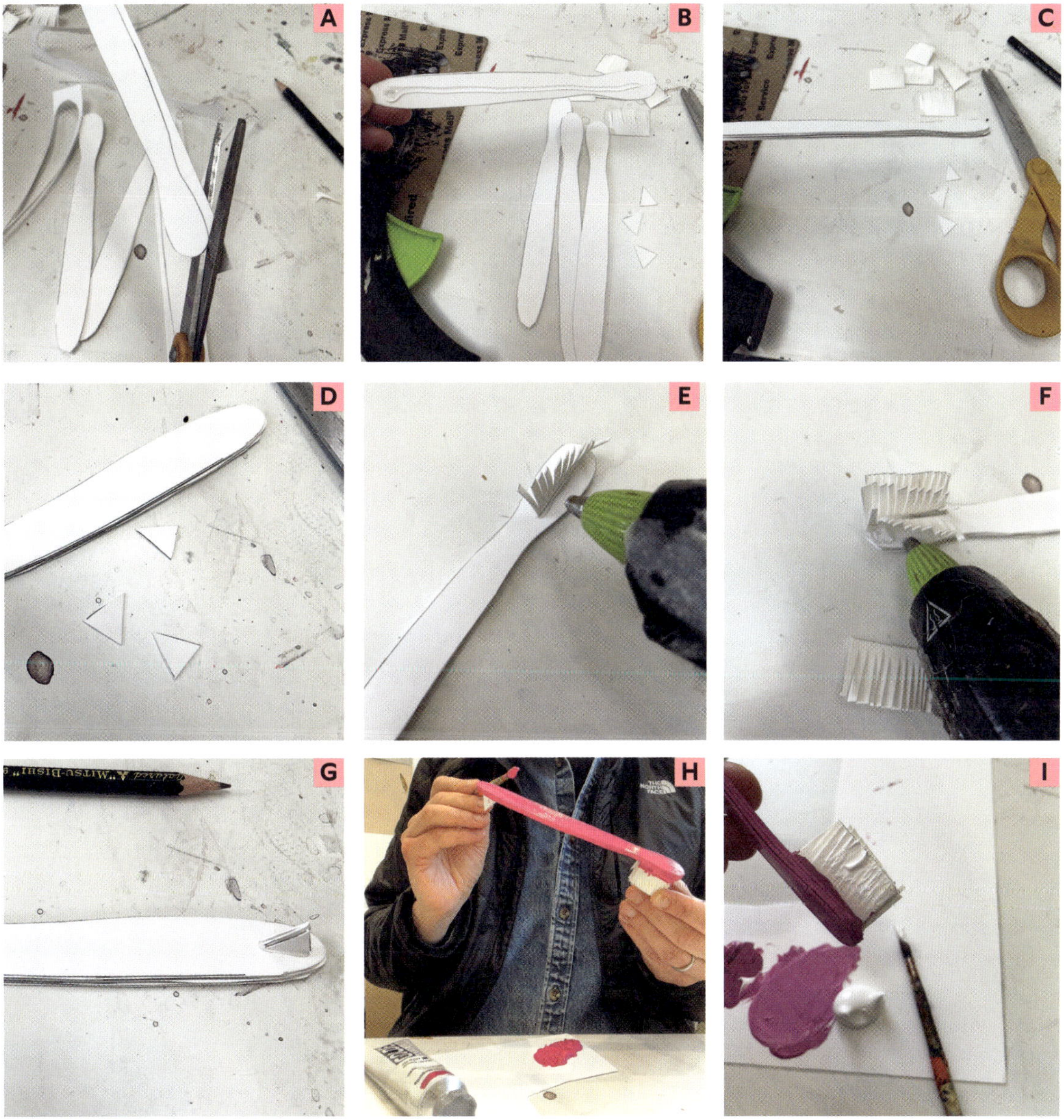

A

B

C

D

E

F

G

H

I

12 Once the bristles are fully dry, use your thin liner brush and paint thin grey lines in the white to add more depth. (J, K, L)

13 Mix some white and pink to make a lighter pink and paint the back toothpick triangle piece on the brush. (M)

14 Once the handle is fully dry, use black and paint CHANEL.

15 Paint a gold circle on the handle.

16 Paint a forward C and then a backwards C in black paint over the gold circle to complete the CHANEL logo. (N)

17 Paint a black outline on the whole toothbrush. (O)

18 Now you have yourself a CHANEL paper toothbrush.

19 Make one for a friend!

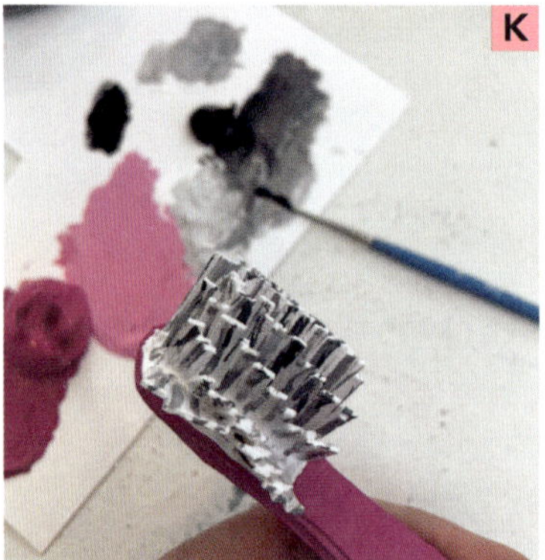

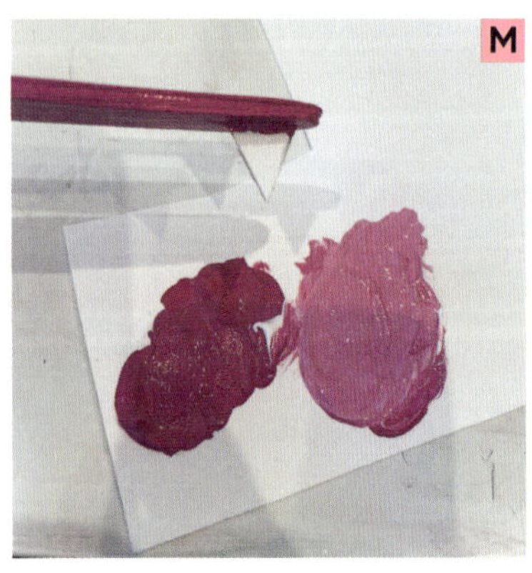

Libby Black is a painter, drawer, and sculptural installation artist living in Berkeley, California. Her artwork charts a path through personal history and a broader cultural context to explore the intersection of politics, feminism, LGBTQ+ identity, consumerism, addiction, notions of value, and desire. She has exhibited nationally and internationally, with such shows as *California Love* at Galerie Droste in Wupertal, Germany; *Bay Area Now 4* at Yerba Buena Center for the Arts; *California Biennial* at the Orange County Museum of Art; and at numerous galleries in New York, Los Angeles, and San Francisco. Black has been an artist-in-residence at Headlands Center for the Arts in Sausalito, CA; Montalvo Arts Center in Saratoga, CA; and Spaces in Cleveland, OH. Her work has been reviewed in *Artforum*, *Art in America*, *ARTnews*, *Flash Art*, and *The New York Times*. She received a BFA from the Cleveland Institute of Art in 1999 and an MFA at the California College of the Arts in 2001. Libby is an Associate Professor at San Francisco State University and is represented by Anthony Meier. You can see more of her work at www.libbyblack.com and @libblack on Instagram.

RED: Block-Printed Tea Towel

CREATED BY

Jen Hewett

"Over a decade ago, I went to Istanbul for the first time. I walked all over the city, under the intense September Mediterranean sun. Thankfully, there were street vendors on almost every corner selling fresh pomegranate juice. Using just a manual press, a mesh strainer, bottled water, and fresh pomegranates, vendors would make a refreshing cup of juice in the most vivid shade of magenta red. This was just enough to cool and fuel me for a few blocks, when, withered from the heat, I'd stop again for another cup of fresh juice. When I think of the color red, I often think about my time in Turkey, when I enjoyed multiple cups of pomegranate juice under the most brilliant blue skies."

Block printing has its roots in Asia. The earliest known prints, from China, date from over four thousand years ago. Wood was carved to create blocks of texts that were then printed using ink. The technique spread to India by the twelfth century where it was, and still is, used to create intricate patterns on paper and fabrics. Even wallpaper has been printed using blocks. Once modern printing techniques were invented and became widespread in use, block printing became more of an artistic practice than a practical one. Although there are still places and people who make textile and paper yardage via hand block-printing.

While traditionally blocks were made of regional woods, print-makers eventually turned to linoleum because it was easier to carve and run through a printing press. Today blocks of rubbery materials are readily available and even easier to carve than their linoleum counterparts. Water-based inks, carving tools, and paints are also easily procured by anyone wanting to try their hand at block printing.

A satisfying way to quickly make multiples on paper or cloth, block printing has grown in popularity in recent years. Blocks can even be carved from simple erasers. It's also an easy medium to expand—using multiple blocks or the same one on repeat—so you can fill a larger space fairly speedily.

MATERIALS

- Pencil—softer pencils are best
- Tracing paper
- Soft block (*not* linoleum)—Speedball easy cut or similar rubber-like blocks are best and easiest to use
- Linoleum cutter tool—many brands offer sets with interchangeable blades
- Paint trim roller or brayer
- 8-ounce (227 g) jar of screen-printing ink for fabric, or fabric paint
- Small (4-by-6- or 8-by-10-inch / 10 by 15 or 20 by 25 cm) acrylic or plexiglass board OR a plastic plate to roll the ink onto
- Cotton dish towel, ironed
- Quilt batting or felt the size of your dish towel (optional) to place between your table and your dish towel
- Template (shown here at 100%)

TEMPLATE

INSTRUCTIONS

1. Place your tracing paper on top of the pomegranate template (you can copy or scan the template onto a loose sheet to make this step easier).

2. Using your pencil, trace the image exactly as it appears. Shade in all the black areas well. You want your pencil marks to be as dark as possible. (A)

3. Next, transfer the image onto your block by placing the tracing paper, pencil side down, on top of the block. (B)

4. Move your fingers (or use a spoon) over the back of the tracing paper. (C) This will transfer your penciled sketch onto the block. (D) Your block will be larger than the sketch. That's fine. We'll trim away the excess later.

5. Insert a #2 or larger blade into your cutting tool. Don't use the #1 tool—it won't carve deeply enough on this soft block. Begin by carving along the outside of the image. (E) Carve away any negative space so that only the pencil sketched area remains. Take your time, and use smooth strokes. Rotate and move the block as you work.

6. Once you've carved along the outside, carve the interior of the image so that only the details that will print remain (aka your pencil marks). (F)

7. Using an X-ACTO or utility knife, trim away the excess block. (G) I like to leave at least 0.25 inch (6 mm) between the edge of the image and the edge of the block. This makes the block easier to hold once it's inked. Clean off the pencil with your finger, an eraser, wet cloth, or baby wipe – otherwise it might blend with your ink or end up on your print. (H)

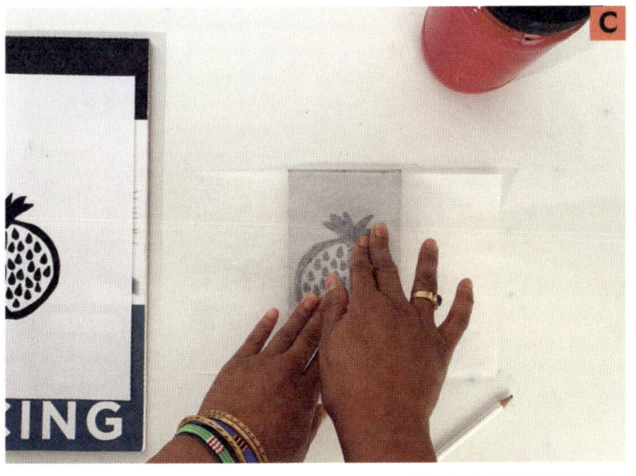
C

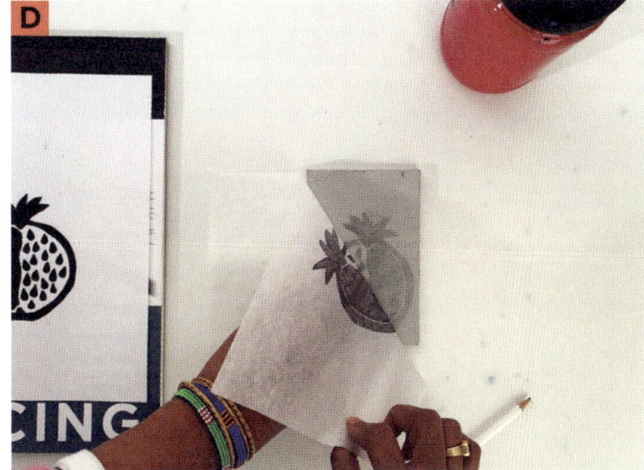
D

E

F

G

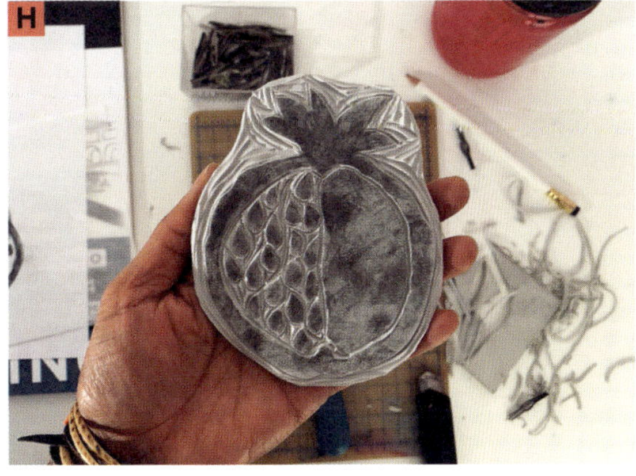
H

8 Place your batting or felt onto your table (if using), then lay your dish towel on top of it. The side you plan to print on should be the side that's closest to and facing you.

9 Put about a tablespoon of screen-printing ink or fabric paint onto your acrylic sheet or plate. (I)

10 Using your paint trim roller or brayer, roll it over your ink until the roller is evenly coated, but not gloppy with ink. (J, K)

11 Roll the ink onto your block, until the block is evenly coated. (L) Be careful not to use pressure. You don't want to force the ink into the carved areas.

12 If you want to test your block, print on a scrap piece of paper first. This will allow you to see if there's any area of your block you'd like to clean up. If an area in the background, or in your shape, printed and you don't want it to, carve it away.

13 Place your block, inked side down, onto the center of the bottom edge of your dish towel. (M) I prefer to begin printing in the center, then work my way out, to ensure that the print is evenly spaced.

14 Using the palms of your hands—not your fingers!—apply pressure to the back of the block to transfer the ink onto the towel. (N) You can use a big spoon to apply pressure as well. Lift the block. You've made your first print! (O)

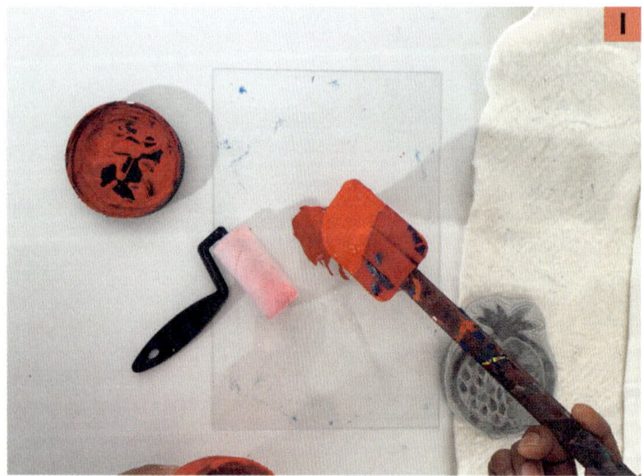
I

J

K

L
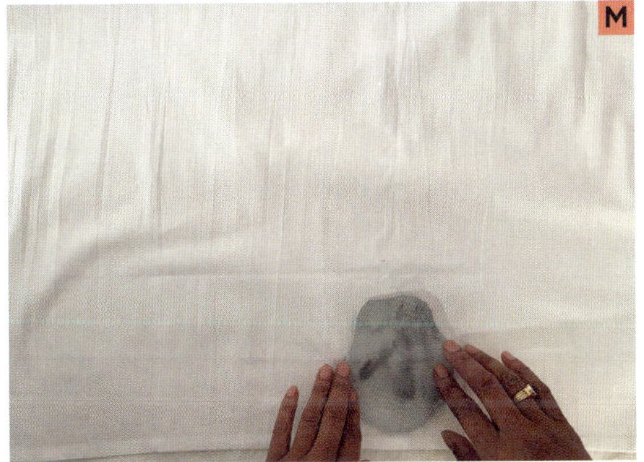
M
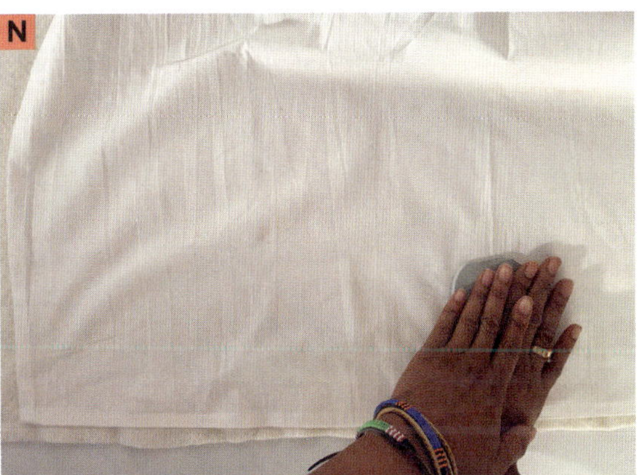
N
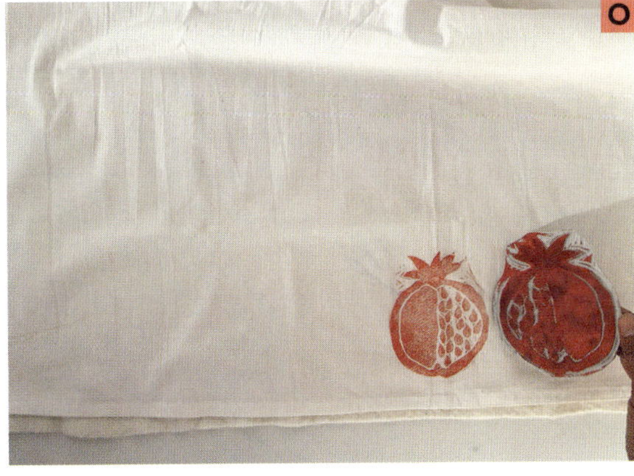
O

15 Continue by printing on the left and right corners of your towel, re-inking the block each time. (P)

16 You can experiment by rotating the print upside down to create a second row. (Q) Or randomly fill up your towel.

17 Allow the ink to dry completely, then iron it on the reverse side on the highest heat setting for three minutes to heat set the ink. Your dish towel is now ready to be used!

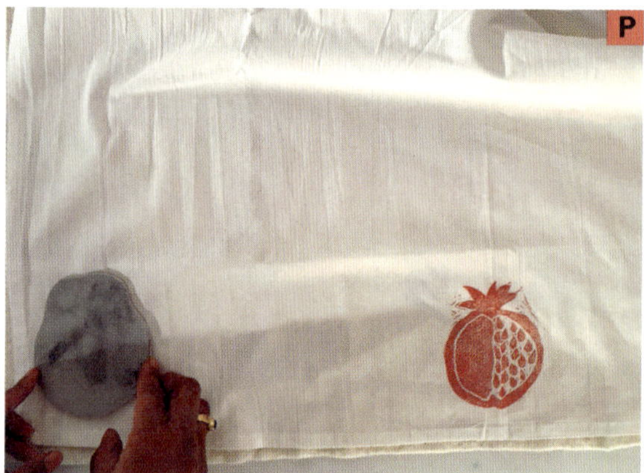
P

Q

Jen Hewett is a printmaker, surface designer, textile artist, and author based in the Hudson Valley. Jen's work combines her love of loud prints, 1970s maximalism, and saturated colors with the textures and light of the landscapes that surround her. In addition to creating her own products, Jen designs fabric for the quilting and home sewing market, and home collections for national manufacturers and retailers. Her clients include: Moda Fabrics, World Market, Anthropologie, Blue Sky Planners, and Brewster Home Fashions. She is the author of *Print, Pattern, Sew* and *This Long Thread: Women of Color on Craft, Community and Connection*. Visit her website at jenhewett.com, her shop at shop.jenhewett.com and her Instagram at @jenhewett.

DARK RED: Needle-Felted Mouth

CREATED BY

Risa Iwasaki Culbertson

"Emotions come out in my facial expressions when words are hard to come by. This continuing series of mouths is my way of celebrating the language and connections of the heart. To create and release them out into the world in honor of the emotions we may hide, long to have seen, love in one another, and capture in moments of joy for just a little bit longer. It serves as a personal reminder to never take a smile for granted, and I hope anyone who views it will be reminded of that, too.

The definition feels so blurred between art and craft, and is debated by artists and craftspeople, but it's two sides of the same coin. Whatever differences there are should be opportunities to learn, collaborate, and grow our own practice. Bringing in different techniques and expressions of emotion are ways to enhance the stories we're trying to share."

Needle felting is a process whereby one uses special notched needles to sculpt raw wool (called roving) into shapes. You literally repeatedly stab the roving—placed atop a soft padded foam block surface—and the needles force the fibers to interlock and become firmer. While the material of felt itself—mostly generated through a wet process of melding fibers together with water and soap—has been used for centuries (to give you a sense: sheep were domesticated in 5000 to 7000 BCE), the art of needle felting is relatively new. We have David and Eleanor Stanwood to thank for inventing the technique in the 1980s.

Needle felting has sculptural qualities. The continued process of thousands of stabbing motions allows one to generate not only perfect spheres and shapes, but also abstract amorphous things as well. The felt lends itself to mimicking fur, fuzz, and other textures we associate with nature. Its malleability allows for easy correction and change of course (unlike marble where if you take out the wrong chunk you can't put it back). It can also be translated into flat, yet dimensional, items that can sit on walls or tables, or even on garments.

The felting process also allows people to easily shift and transition between colors—mimicking painting in its blending ability. One can also decide to very tightly or more loosely felt something, based on desired effect. Many find the repetitive process of stabbing the roving quite therapeutic too, just watch your fingers as the needles are sharp!

MATERIALS

- 12-by-12-by-4-inch (30 by 30 by 10 cm) recycled foam block (see resources, below)
- Carving tool—I prefer a hot wire cutter with multiple attachments but a box cutter or an electric turkey knife would work
- Felting needles—I use a multi needle tool (see resources, below) in addition to a single or double needle tool for details. Have a few extras on hand in case they break. I use sizes 36 triangle for the majority of the project and 38 triangle for the finishing touches. The 38 triangle is a general all-purpose needle if you're wanting to just get one type.
- Carding brush to help blend (optional; you can also do this with your hands)
- Wire or hook and glue for mounting
- Roving wool (see resources, below)
    - For blending: 3 ounces (or approx. 170 inches / 4.3 m) red, 2 ounces (or approx. 115 inches / 2.9 m) wine or burgundy, pinch of black
    - No blending: 3 ounces (or approx. 170 inches / 4.3 m) dark red
    - 14 inches (36 cm) white (2 ounces or approx. 115 inches / 2.9 m if you are using white roving for your teeth as well)
    - 14 inches (36 cm) black
    - 1 ounce (or approx. 55 inches / 1.4 m) of white core wool for teeth base (optional—core wool is thicker and builds up faster, but you can just use your white roving instead, just add to your overall quantity of white)
    - Pinch of pink roving (optional)

RESOURCES

- Foam blocks: Yoga blocks and polystyrene (similar to floral arranging bricks) are good alternatives, but check your local art supply reuse store, or local businesses for shipment packaging. Smaller pieces can be glued together using UHU expanded polystyrene glue.
- Multi-needle felting tool: https://clover-usa.com/products/felting-needle-tool
- Roving wool and felting needles: https://wistyria.com

INSTRUCTIONS

1 Map out your mouth. Using a sharpie, draw directly onto a clean and dry foam block. (A) You can freehand this or project/print an image and trace onto the surface.

2 Mark out three layers: first layer (lips), second layer (teeth), and third layer (inside of mouth). The third layer is going to be the most recessed and require the most carving while the first layer will be more shaped than cut into. Take a mirror out and use your own mouth as a guide for depth.

3 Work from the biggest cuts to details. Start by cutting around the outside of the mouth creating the silhouette. (B)

4 Little by little shave into the outer lip line to create the overall mouth shape. Stay mindful as this is the top layer; you want to maximize the depth of your block. But, lips are not flat, you'll want to angle down to the narrow parts of the mouth, and the sides will need to be shaved and rounded.

5 Once you're happy with the outer line, dive into the teeth/second layer. Carving little gaps between teeth will allow more detail and depth at the felting stage.

6 The inside of the mouth is the final/third layer and one requiring the deepest carving. Make sure it's recessed deeper than the teeth but not so deep that it goes through to the other side of your foam block. (C)

7 Keep shaving off and cutting until you sculpt a form you're happy with. No need to worry if things aren't smooth, it's all going to be under a blanket of wool so bolder cuts are going to show better than detailed work.

8 Fuzz prep! (D) This is only if you're blending wool colors. If you aren't planning on this, perhaps try a little bit anyways! Using the carding tool, brush light red and dark burgundy roving together. Brush in opposite directions. Pull the roving off the brush and repeat. Repeat until blended. Blended colors offer more depth and color shifts that mimic painting techniques. (E)

9 You can achieve blending without carding by simply mixing the colors by hand—pulling and scrunching the roving until fully blended.

10 Let the felting begin. New to felting? Have no fear! Keep your felting needle straight (bending will increase the chances of breaking). Keep your fingers out of harm's way, and push the wool into the foam. Go deep enough to clear the barbs on the tips of your needle and until you see the fibers stick to your form.

11 Using a single needle or your double needle tool, with a coarse 38 triangle size, start with the insides of the mouth/third layer. Take a tuff of black by pinching the end of the roving wool and gently pulling. The roving should be dense enough to cover the form underneath but thin enough to see some light come through if you hold it up. Lay it over the form and start felting. Repeat the process of pulling wool, laying it down, and felting until the foam underneath is no longer visible. Bring in smaller pulls of black between the teeth as well. (F) It's ok for things to look fuzzy at this point, because you'll be doing a final felt later on.

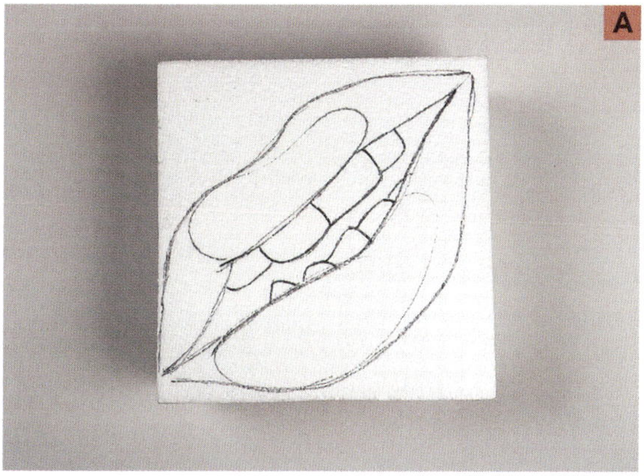

A
B 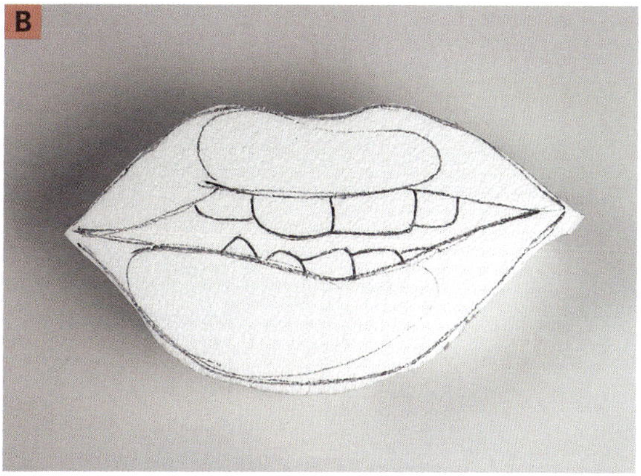
C 
D 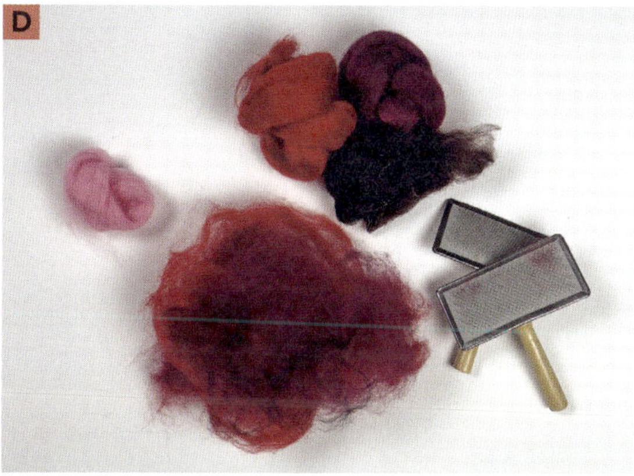
E 
F

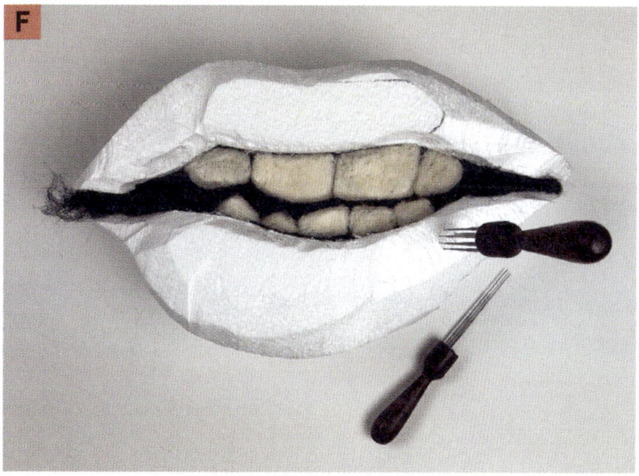

12 Repeat this technique for the second layer, teeth. Use the optional core wool to create a thicker layer for this section or simply use white roving wool. As you layer and felt, the black wool between the teeth will blend and soften the contrast becoming more subtle instead of a full gap. Round the corners by moving your needle around the curve while being mindful to not bend your needle.

13 On the top layer/lips cover the biggest parts in one color. (G) Use the lighter shade of red until the foam lips are fully covered.

14 With smaller tuffs, begin fanning the fibers to thin them out so they become more transparent. Bring darker shades in spots shadows would hit and lighter ones (for example if you have pink) for highlights. Lay, felt, and repeat until you achieve your desired look. (H, I, J)

15 Glue a hook or twist a wire in the back for easy hanging.

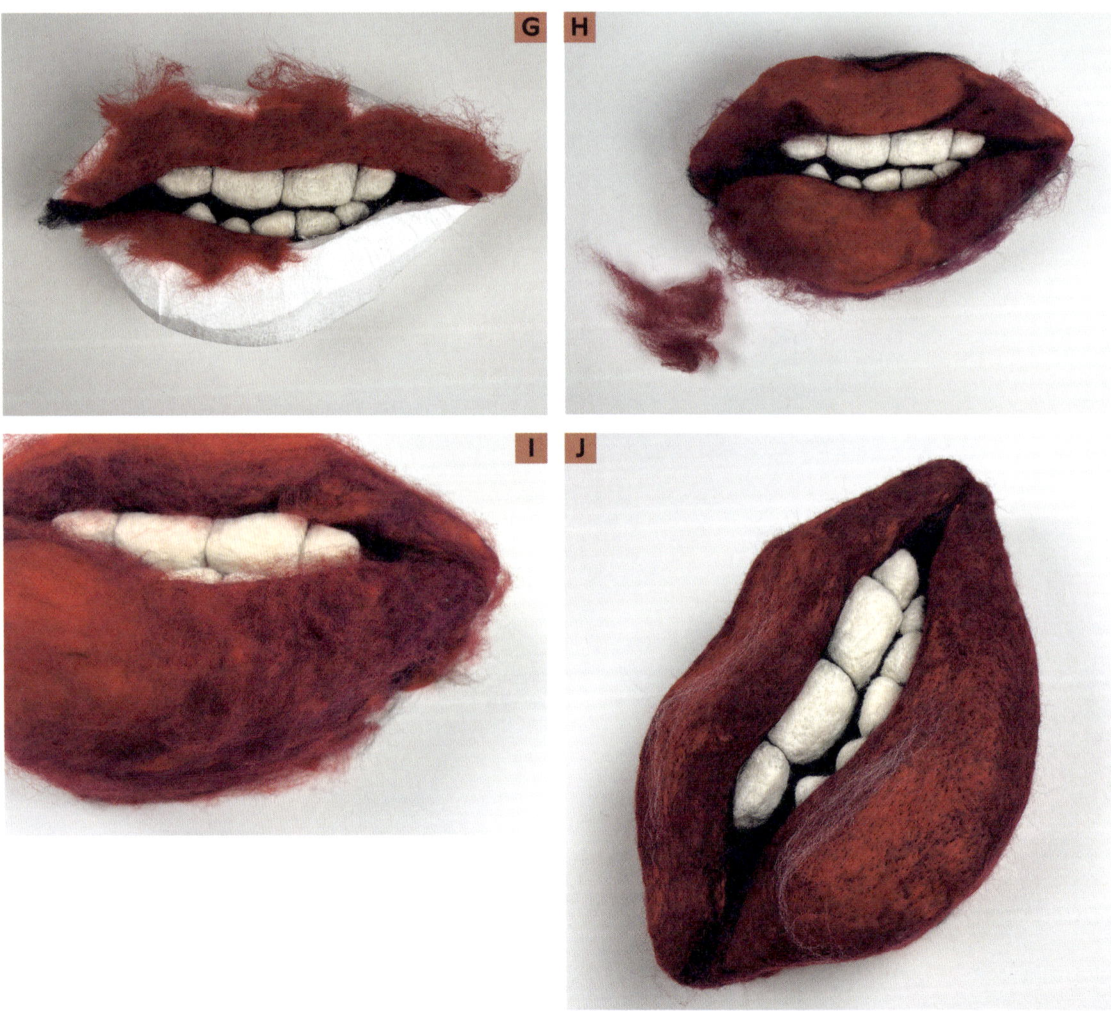

Risa Iwasaki Culbertson is a multi-disciplinary artist living in San Francisco, California, with a love of fiber arts, illustrating, and storytelling. Biracial and born in Japan, she grew up creating art to bridge the gap between her two worlds. Inspired by the healing and connective power of humor and play, she creates her wacky, whimsical, and colorful work as a way to process deep emotions, create places of belonging, and find ways to stay connected to those we love. Visit her Instagram: @Risa_Iwasaki_Culbertson or website: www.RisaCulbertson.com.

ORANGE: Botanical Swatches

CREATED BY
Ana Bianchi

"Am I a florist? No, but I sure love the shapes and colors of flowers. Is this a flower arrangement? Not really, for me it is more like a blob of color. This is how I discover and experiment with color. It is the result of something I call abstract naturalism. Let me explain. . .

I have always been color-obsessed. Every day, everywhere, I go about color-harvesting. I look for colors in nature, in things, in the clothes of people I see in the street, or the produce in the market. I search for intriguing colors, or interesting combinations. I notice them, observe them, and make mental notes. My head is full of those color notes! But then there are times when I go out on a color mission—to find deep chromatic blacks; or very pale, almost white hues. Or to find the whole range of a specific color, like the orange in these pages—from the lightest to the deepest—from its closest point to yellow and to as close as possible to red. When I'm on such a mission, I find and gather flowers, fruits, leaves, or anything in nature with the right hue or tone needed for my search. I see these objects as ready-made color swatches provided by Mother Nature. I collect them, group them, and photograph them.

Why do I experiment with color like this? First, because the search sharpens my eye and the act of careful observation centers my mind. But mostly because I discover rich, interesting colors and color combinations. There is no need to mix paint! Mother Nature already mixed all kinds of hues for me to learn from! (Also, I thoroughly enjoy playing with my botanical subjects while photographing them). From the photos, I can abstract chromatic combinations I may not have considered before. And a single photo can render many palettes. I use these color palettes in paintings, crafts, graphic design projects, in the clothes I wear, or in my home. The more I color-harvest, the more color love *I find."*

Flower arranging has been with us for a very long time. The first evidence of flowers in vases appear on wall carvings in Egypt from 2500 BCE. The Greeks and Romans actually *cultivated* flowers for decorative purposes—although they were much more drawn to wreaths or garlands than vases. The Chinese used flowers on Buddhist, Taoist, and Confucian altars, and depicted flowers in embroidery, paintings, and wood carvings. The Japanese developed Ikebana—a minimalist approach using asymmetry and simplicity to invoke a strong emotional response. In the Middle Ages, monks created flower arrangements from the gardens they tended. Across cultures, flowers have symbolic meaning—peonies for good fortune, chrysanthemums for royalty and resilience, water lilies for the goddess Isis.

In the seventeenth and eighteenth centuries, Dutch painters painstakingly created lush canvases of impossible floral arrangements—impossible because they contained flowers that could never be blooming at the same time. As living bouquets can do, these paintings often conveyed messages of beauty, mystery, life and death, and even morality. In 1883, confined to bed and approaching death, Manet painted sixteen deceptively simple bouquets. These stunning and intimate paintings show a depth of skill and emotion that set the tone for contemporary floral still lifes to come.

We'd be hard pressed to attend an event—any party, wedding, funeral, banquet—and not see flowers somewhere. Flowers accompany all our important rites of passage (prom!) and help declare emotional states we sometimes have trouble articulating. We are often obsessed with or calmed by our own or other people's gardens or even by individual flowers. Flowers delight us with their beauty and fragrance; they allow us to bring a bit of nature into our worlds, enriching our surroundings and providing moments of wonder and joy.

MATERIALS

- Wide variety of botanical material: flowers, fruits, leaves, twigs, etc.
- Camera–any kind will suffice, from your phone to a professional camera
- White board
- Pad of watercolor paper
- Art materials of your choice: watercolor, pastels, gouache, colored pencils

INSTRUCTIONS

My color-harvesting practice consists of three parts: Observe > Analyze > Create.

Observe

1 As a warmup, start by going for a walk in nature or sitting in your garden and tune into a color that first catches your eye—a flower, a leaf, a lichen, a mossy rock. From there, notice other colors nearby and how they relate to each other and how you feel about them, what you like.

2 If the garden is yours or the place where you are walking allows for it, start collecting "botanical swatches." No access to a garden? No problem, you can also just go to a flower shop or market (fruits and veggies are also great swatches!) and color-harvest there. If nature isn't your cup of tea, use things you find in your drawers: threads, buttons, little toys, and trinkets.

3 The point is to gather a wide variety of smallish bits of natural or human-made color that have caught your eye. Spread them on a tray or table so that you can observe them well.

Analyze

1 Once I have that day's color harvest, I start to play and discover possibilities. I begin arranging the elements in groups and place them on a whiteboard. I proceed by combining things I like together in that moment. I snap a picture. I reorganize and subtract, or add new elements and shoot again. (A, B) Sometimes one photo is all I need; sometimes I create many compositions. Pay attention to your intuition and ask yourself questions like:

Why do I like this combination?

Do these colors/objects work next to each other? How are they interacting?

Is there enough contrast? Is it interesting enough? Is this a combination I have never used?

What is working here and what is not?

2 Keep shooting photos until you have exhausted the possibilities. It is in asking these questions as you photograph that will sharpen your eye and take you to a novel color place in your art and craft. Do these images need to be fine art, gallery-level pro photographs? No, but they can be. These are color studies for your own process, to inform your art or your craft.

3 I prefer photographing on white to keep the focus on the botanicals (or trinkets); but you can also play with changing the background color which will add one more layer of color experimentation.

4 I always set up everything as a flat lay, photographing completely perpendicular to the board from above.

A

B

5 I shoot with natural, indirect light since it renders the colors better and prevents harsh shadows. This is also simple, as I can shoot anywhere if it is daytime. If you have the equipment, you can set up indoors with artificial studio lights and diffusers. Whatever photographing setup you use, what matters is that it renders a natural image that truly reflects the colors of the original items cleanly.

6 If the photo needs adjustment, I advise quick retouches to your photo with something like Adobe Photoshop or Snapseed on your phone to adjust the exposure, make the background clean white, and adjust colors as close to the real subject as possible.

7 Once you have your photo(s), pull out the art materials. Observe the photo and, analyzing the whole image, locate a small area of interest. Create a color palette on paper using your materials of choice—paints you can mix, like watercolors, work especially well. (C) Mix or layer color with the intention of being as accurate as possible to what you are seeing in the photo. Your palette can have as few as three colors or as many as ten or twelve–simply assure that your choices are pleasing to your eye. Trust your instinct. Make as many of these paper palettes as you wish. Collect them as color index cards for immediate or future use.

Create

1 Pick one of your palettes and use it in a creative project of your choice! Let it guide your choice of threads or fabric in sewing or embroidery or serve as a limited color palette for an illustration or painting. The more you practice with color and develop your sense of palettes, the more interesting and beautiful your craft or art will be.

Originally from Mexico, **Ana Bianchi** is an artist, designer, illustrator, and children's book author/illustrator. With degrees in graphic design and fine arts, her more than thirty-five years of creative work spans disciplines ranging from printmaking and ceramics to illustration, surface design, and children's wear to graphic design and branding for clients small and big, from local restaurants to major airlines. Her art brand, AnaLovesColor, is where all these diverse projects live. Her lifelong love of color is what connects it all and helps her comfortably move from one discipline to another and from one technique to another. Her book *Color Curious: Find Color Inspiration All Around You for Art, Design, and Life* illustrates ideas and inspiration around a variety of color themes. When not working in her Bay Area studio, Ana loves to cook and bake colorful things, tend to her garden (her other color studio), and spend time with her tiny family: Alberto, her husband; Florencia, her daughter; and Bonnie and PepaPug, their dogs. To see her work visit AnaLovesColor.com and @analovescolor on Instagram, and join her mailing list for more color love and to learn about upcoming presentations, products, and the latest colorful art.

TANGERINE: Segment Skirt

CREATED BY

Sonya Philip

"This sewing project uses French Seams to creates ridges which usually remain unseen on the inside of a garment. But instead, in this skirt, the seams become part of the design—a way to accentuate its citrus-like segments. The size of this simple skirt is determined by the number of segments used, in combination with the length of the elastic. A waistband is made after sewing the pieces together."

There are several things in our lives that were once handmade and then became mass produced—like garments. As we've become accustomed to running out to buy clothing at a multitude of stores, making one's own clothing by hand has become something that some people gravitate towards, both as a means to be creative and as a way to counter mass consumerism. Not only has slow fashion become a concept that more people know about and want to practice, but challenges like Me Made May (originally started as Me Made March in 2010 by Zoe Edwards), in which people wear and document wearing their homemade clothes for the month of May, have sprung up to support and encourage this effort.

Sewing one's own clothes allows for a lot more freedom. Want mismatched pockets? An asymmetrical hemline? Upholstery fabric for a shirt? No problem! While there are plenty of sewing techniques that require a sewing machine and some know-how, there are also ways to sew that novices can explore.

Sewing is, of course, not limited to garments or household items. Plenty of artists (like Lauren DiCioccio) are exploring sewn soft sculptures and other fine art forms. There is something particularly satisfying about wearing something handmade though! Especially if we add a personal touch like a statement pocket or a special seam.

MATERIALS

- Mid-weight linen, cotton, or natural fiber blend*
  - Small to Large: 2 yards (1.8 m)
  - X-Large: 2⅝ yards (2.4 m)
- 1 inch (2.5 cm) non-roll elastic
  - 22 to 45 inches (55 to 114 cm) depending on waist size
- Pins or wonder clips
- Large safety pin
- Sewing machine with matching or contrasting thread/bobbin
- Hand sewing needle
- Pattern (see pages 82-83) copied or scanned and enlarged to 125%

*Something to consider when choosing fabric: due to the way the pattern is cut out, prints with strong vertical orientation will require more fabric unless the fabric is on the wider side and you're using matching thread (using thread in a slightly lighter or darker color makes segments stand out).

SIZES

WAIST MEASUREMENT

Small: 28 to 32 inches (71 to 81 cm)

Medium: 35 to 39 inches (89 to 99 cm)

Large: 42 to 46 inches (1 to 1.2 m)

X-Large: 49 to 53 inches (1.2 to 1.3 m)

PATTERN

The Segment Skirt top and bottom pieces are shown at reduced size here. Enlarge 125% on a copier or scanner to get to 100% size.

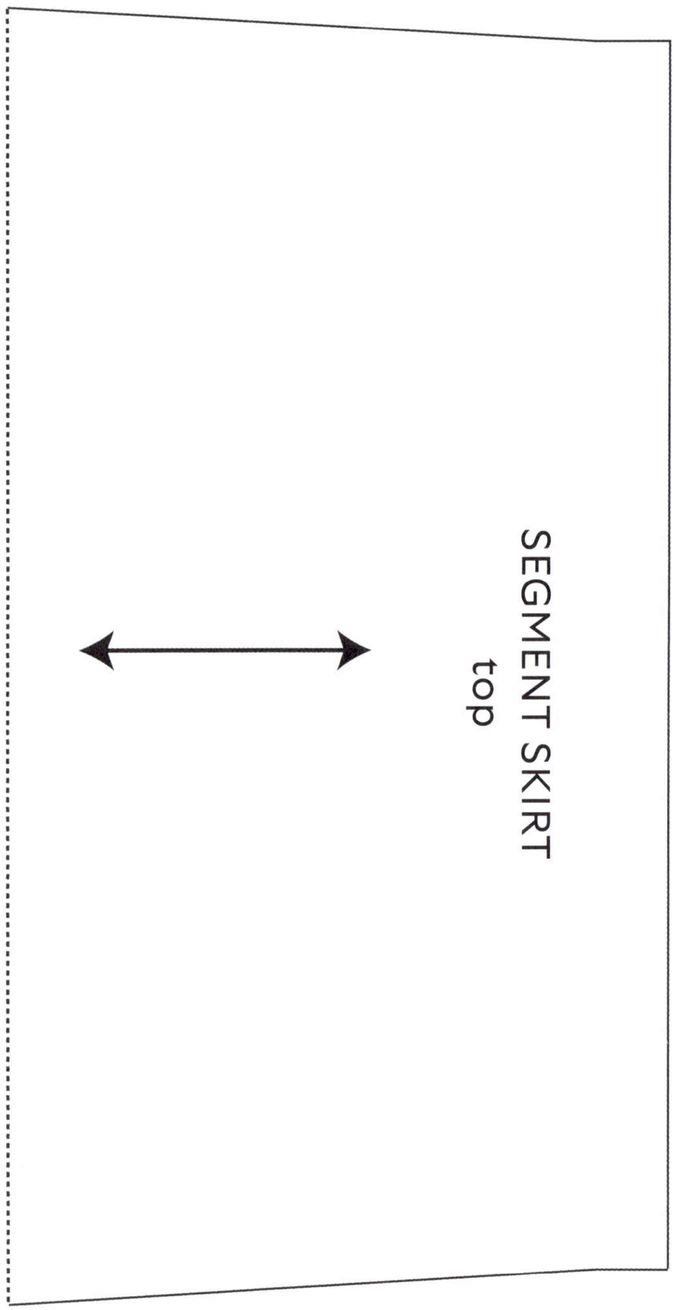

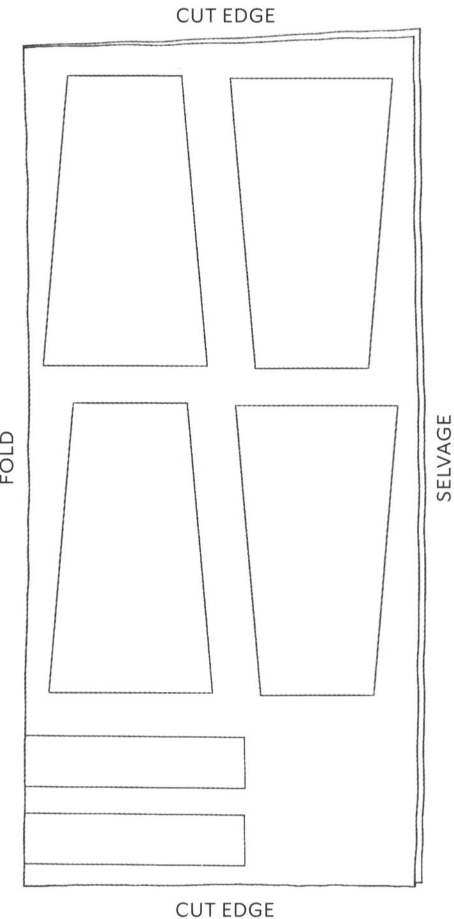

SEGMENT SKIRT
top

SEGMENT SKIRT
bottom

INSTRUCTIONS

1 Copy or scan pattern, enlarging to 125%, and cut out. Measure along the dotted line and mark the middle of each piece. Lay the top pattern piece on a sheet of paper, tape it down, and measure 14 inches (36 cm) down from the middle. Make a mark and center the bottom pattern piece. Tape and draw two diagonal lines to connect the top and bottom. (A) (It's possible to lengthen or shorten but remember any modifications will change the amount of fabric required.)

2 Fold the fabric in half vertically, selvages together. Place the segment pattern piece on top of fabric, close to but not on the fold. Weight and trace with chalk. This will create two segment pieces. Flip the pattern piece upside down and trace another pair of segments. (B) (If making a size with an odd number of segments, simply unfold fabric, then trace and cut out a piece on a single layer of fabric. With wider fabric, flipping the pattern piece is not necessary.) Trace the number of segments needed for your size. Small: six segments; Medium: seven segments; Large: eight segments; X-Large: nine segments. Reserve fabric for the waistband.

3 To avoid sewing the pieces together incorrectly, it might help to mark the narrower top part of each piece with chalk. (C) Starting with two segment pieces, match them together at the top and bottom. Pin along the side with right sides together. Take note that this is opposite to how French Seams are usually sewn. Sew using ¼ inch (6 mm) seam allowance. Continue joining all the pieces until they form a tube. (D)

4 After sewing all the segments, use a rotary cutter or scissors to trim the edges of each seam to ⅛ inch (3 mm). Take care to not to cut too close to stitches. (E) Fold along the seam, so the wrong sides are together, press and pin or clip to hold fold in place. (F) Sew a second seam, using a scant ¼ inch (6 mm) seam allowance. (G) Repeat for each seam on every segment. Press all the seam ridges so they lay in the same direction.

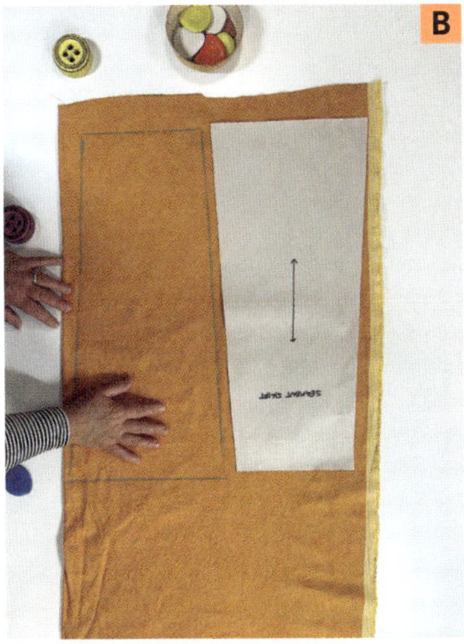

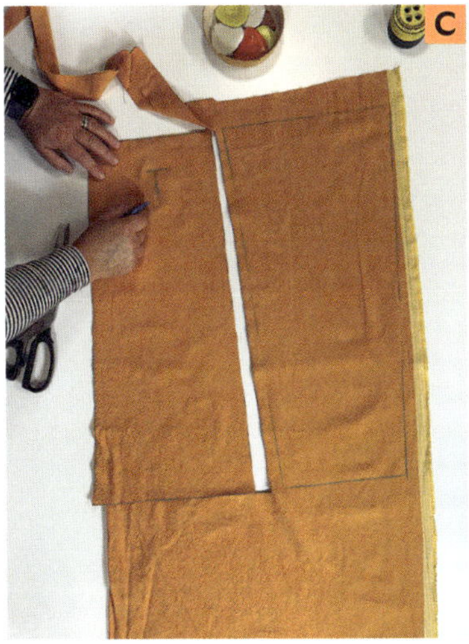

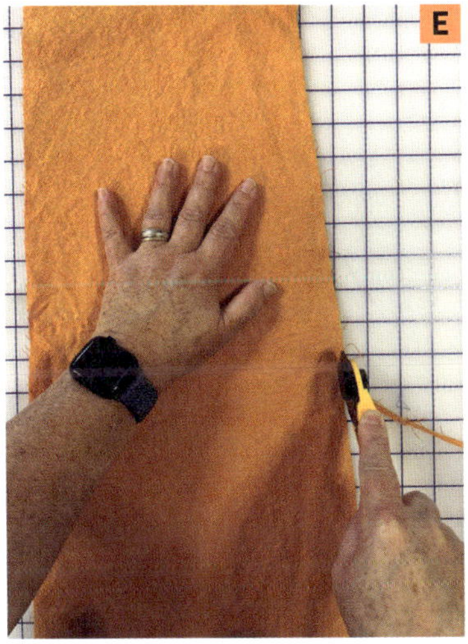

5 Measure for the waistband. After joining all the segments, lay the skirt flat. Measure across the top. (H) Round up to the nearest whole number and add 1 inch (2.5 cm), then divide this number in half, this is the waistband measurement. For example, top measurement: 26 inches (66 cm); add 1 inch (2.5 cm), 27 inches (68.5 cm); then divide in half 13.5 inches (34 cm).

6 Next cut out the waistband. Fold the remaining fabric in half. Use chalk and a ruler to draw a horizontal line using the waistband measurement. Then measure down 3.5 inches (9 cm) and mark, repeat once more in the middle. Connect the marks by drawing a second horizontal line. Draw a short vertical line to form a rectangle. Repeat and cut out. This will create two waistband pieces. (I)

7 With right sides together, pin the short edges of the waistband together and sew using ½ inch (1.5 cm) seam allowance. Press the edges of the seam open. Fold one of the short edges ¼ inch (6 mm) to the wrong side. To attach the waistband to the skirt, position the waistband at the top so the right sides are together. The right side of the skirt will be the side with the seam ridges. Starting with the end with the folded over edge, pin the waistband around the top of the skirt. When you reach the end, overlap the waistband and pin together. Make sure to leave at least ½ inch (1.5 cm) of waistband fabric. (J)

8 Sew around the waistband, using ½ inch (1.5 cm) seam allowance. Press the waistband and seam edges up towards the unsewn edge of the waistband. Next, fold and press the unsewn edge of the waistband ¼ inch (6 mm) to the wrong side. (K) Fold the waistband over a second time to the inside, positioning the edge so it overlaps the line of stitches. Press and pin in place. (L) Sew around the waistband, keeping stitches close to the edge of the waistband fold. (M)

9 Measure out a piece of elastic about 4 to 6 inches (10 to 15 cm) less than the waist measurement. Test it by holding it around your waist. Then attach a large safety pin to one end of the elastic and slip it into the gap in the waistband. (N)

H
I
J
K
L
M
N

10 Work the elastic through the waistband, then pull out both ends of the elastic and remove the safety pin. Feel all along the waistband to make sure the elastic hasn't twisted and make adjustments if necessary. Overlap the edges ½ inch (1.5 cm) and sew together. Sew back and forth several times. (O)

11 Try the skirt on to check the fit of the elastic, then thread the hand sewing needle to close the gap in the waistband. (P) Distribute the gathers evenly along the elastic.

12 Finally, finish the edge of the skirt by making a double fold over hem. First fold the edge over ¼ inch (6 mm) to the wrong side and press. Then make a second ½ inch (1.5 cm) fold. Press, pin in place, and sew. (It's easier to sew from behind the seam ridge, so the presser foot doesn't get caught.) (Q)

Sonya Philip is an artist, designer, and teacher. She received an MFA in Creative Writing from Mills College and a BFA from the University of California, Santa Cruz. In 2012, she started a project called 100 Acts of Sewing, making dresses while documenting the process. Since then, Sonya has made it her mission to convince people to sew their own clothes, teaching workshops across the country. When not covered in bits of thread, she can be found knitting, gardening, or walking her dogs. Sonya lives in San Francisco with her family. Visit her website www.100actsofsewing.com.

MUSTARD: Quilt

CREATED BY

Robert J. Bosscher

"When I started thinking about this project, I immediately thought of Albers. Not necessarily Josef, although his work on color theory is incredibly influential in art, but his wife Anni, whose work in textiles melds so nicely with my own love of quilting! The two Albers, Anni and Josef, worked together and influenced each other. Their ideas and their art became impactful on the art of the twentieth century, and continue to resonate today. I think it's almost impossible to discuss either Anni or Josef without mentioning the other, due to the way in which each's work informs the other's. Not only did the Alberses bridge art and craft, but their specific ideas around color adjacency really intrigue me as an artist who works in a more traditional craft medium. Color adjacency is the idea that the colors which are placed next to each other in a work of art will impact and appear to change one another. Josef Albers created many studies and painted works that explored this effect, and Anni explored it in her textiles and prints.

Quilts became a great medium to explore these ideas. While color adjacency can be explored with lots of color combinations, I chose to work with colors that have higher contrast, selecting almost complimentary colors. To pair with the mustard colors, I picked a magenta on the warmer side of purple (with a redder tone than a pure purple), which I really liked. It seemed to have more pop than a cooler purple would have—color adjacency magic! Another fun part was searching out the varieties of mustards—warmer and cooler examples to show the breadth of the color and how the appearance of the magenta seems to change depending on which of the mustards surround it. Using a traditional quilt block (the log cabin block) recalled the history of quilting and also very easily created the isolated squares that the Albers used in his color studies."

Since the dawn of fabric and thread, people around the world have created padded cloth for bedding and clothing of all kinds, including armor. The term quilt comes from the Latin *culcita*, meaning a stuffed sack. The word quilt itself is quite interesting as it can be used both as a noun—the three-layered stitched blanket—and a verb—the act of stitching such an object together.

We now recognize the almost infinite possibilities of a quilt, and the immense variety of colors, patterns, and styles of quilting that are practiced across the globe. There are precise and perfectly pieced quilts, quilts that use up any scraps of fabric on hand (from flour sacks to old jeans), and quilts that have way less rhyme and reason (often referred to as "crazy quilts").

Where quilts were once primarily functional, they have now most certainly entered the fine art arena with a number of exhibitions of quilts making their way into modern art museums. The quilts of Gees Bend, Faith Ringgold, Pacita Abad, and Rosie Lee Tompkins are just a few of those that have been deemed "fine art" and graced museum walls. Quilts also have a long tradition of entering the political sphere—from the Abolitionist quilts of the 1800s to the Aids Memorial Quilt of the 1980s. It's easy to see how something so intimate can be the perfect canvas, heirloom, and art piece.

MATERIALS

- FABRIC
  - ½ yard (45.5 cm) of six to eight primary color shade fabrics/mustard

    I started with a nice medium tone fabric, and then selected additional fabrics that were slightly warmer or cooler in tone, or slight shifts in saturation. Solids and tonal print fabrics work best—the more patterned the fabrics tend to be, the less the color adjacency shifts stand out due to the distraction of the print design.

  - ¾ yard (68.5 cm) of contrast color/magenta

    This will be used for both the center square of the blocks as well as the binding of the quilt. I chose a fairly high contrast color that really stood out, but you can absolutely change the feel of the quilt by choosing a contrast color that has less contrast or is a more analogous color.

- BACKING FABRIC
  - You'll need 3 yards (2.5 m) if you are using fabric that is 42 inches (1 m) wide—the backing can be pieced or a wide-back fabric. Use what you have or what you want! Just have a large enough backing so it extends a few inches beyond your quilt top on all sides.

- BATTING
  - Plan on a batting size that extends a few inches on each side of your finished quilt top. This helps give you a little room for shifting when quilting. I used an 80/20 poly-cotton blend, but use whatever batting you'd like!

- THREAD
  - You'll need piecing thread (I use whatever color is already on my machine—usually a neon yellow—but a medium-grey blends well with most fabric colors and is more typical). You'll also need a quilting thread. I chose a mustard quilting thread that matched the top well and blended with the primary color. If you do any hand quilting or special stitching, you'll need thread for that as well.

- TOOLS
  - Rotary cutter
  - Cutting mat
  - Quilting ruler
  - Sewing pins
  - Ironing board and iron
  - Sewing machine
  - Thread snips
  - Basting tools according to your preferred basting method
  - Pressing aid, light spray starch, water spray bottle (optional)

PREPARATION

Fully read through the directions first, as cutting accurately once is better than needing to go find more fabric! (Yes, this advice does come from having experience in not reading thoroughly.)

Some people like to prewash their fabrics before sewing. I don't, but if you feel like you need to or are worried about colors bleeding, do it! Prewashing does mean you will need to press your fabric well before starting to make your cuts.

Directions are assuming a standard fabric width of 42 inches (1 m) and that you are sewing with a standard ¼-inch (6 mm) seam. If you are used to sewing garments, this is a bit smaller than garment seams and a ¼-inch (6 mm) foot for your sewing machine is a great tool to have. The more consistent you can be with your seams, the more consistent your quilt will be and you'll reduce issues of warping or the top not lying flat.

A note on pressing your seams: some people like to press the seams open to reduce bulky layers around the seams. Some people like to press the seams to one side as they feel it strengthens the seams. I do both depending on the project or my mood for the day. You press however you want! I haven't found that it really matters one way or the other.

There are so many great tutorials and how-tos online–way too many to list! If you get stuck, need a different method than I've described, or just a different way of explaining something, a simple Google search will find you multiple videos for whatever you need. When I started quilting, I watched dozens of tutorials, and I still like watching them today! There is always so much to learn and keep learning to find what works best for you.

The finished size of the throw quilt will be 48-by-64 inches (1.2 by 1.6 m); six blocks by eight blocks (blocks finish at 8 inches / 20 cm). The quilt can easily be sized up or down depending on how you want to use it! You will just need to adjust the amount of fabric and batting size.

INSTRUCTIONS

Cut the contrast fabric (magenta).

1 Cut three strips, 2.5 inch (6.5 cm) by the WOF (width of fabric, typically 42 inches / 1 m), from the ¾ yard (69 cm) of the magenta fabric. (A) Set aside the remaining magenta fabric for binding.

2 Sub-cut those three strips into forty-eight 2.5-by-2.5-inch (6.5 by 6.5 cm) squares. (B, C)

Cut the primary fabrics (mustards).

1 Cut five 3.5 inch (9 cm) by the WOF strips from each ½ yard (45.5 cm) cut. (D)

2 Sub-cut strips into following pieces: We'll call them A, B, and C for clarity!

A: eight 2.5-by-3.5-inch (6.5 by 9 cm) rectangles

B: sixteen 5.5-by-3.5-inch (14 by 9 cm) rectangles (E)

C: eight 8.5-by-3.5-inch (21.5 by 9 cm) rectangles

3 Repeat for the remaining primary color (mustard) fabrics—these instructions are if you are using six mustard fabrics. If you use more than six mustard fabrics, you will need to adjust the number of blocks required for each fabric to get to forty-eight total block sets. (F)

Sew the blocks together

1 These can be chain pieced where you sew all centers to the A pieces or you can do each block one at a time if you're worried about keeping everything clear and in order.

2 Sew a magenta square to a 2.5-inch (6.5 cm) side of an A piece. Make sure you are sewing with RST (Right Side of the fabrics Together, this is very important with prints). (G)

3 Press the seam.

4 Turn the pieced unit so the magenta square is on the bottom. Sew one B piece to the 5.5-inch (14 cm) side of your pieced unit, keeping RST. (H, I)

5 Press the seam.

6 Turn the pieced unit 90 degrees counter-clockwise (so the B piece is at the top). Sew the second B piece to the 5.5-inch (14 cm) side of your pieced unit, keeping RST. (J, K)

7 Press the seam.

8 Turn the pieced unit 90 degrees counter-clockwise (second B piece is on top). Sew one C piece to the 8.5-inch (21.5 cm) side of your pieced unit, keeping RST. (L, M)

9 Press the seams.

10 Your block is complete! (N)

11 Repeat for all block units, insuring you're sewing RST, and being consistent in the direction you are turning your pieced units when adding the next piece.

G

H

I

J

K

L

M

N

Assemble the quilt top.

1. I like to play with layout a bit. Arrange your blocks in a six-by-eight grid. (O) Try to keep the same fabrics separate, as that will help with the color adjacency illusion.
2. Rearrange your blocks and try different options—taking photos is a great way to capture options and quickly compare differences.
3. Piece the top.
4. Sew together the blocks in the layout you like.
5. I sew blocks into rows, and then sew rows together.
6. Use pins as needed to align blocks and help seams meet. (P)
7. Once all of the rows are together, press the top so the seams lay flat.

O

P

Baste.

1 This is putting your quilt sandwich together—your backing, batting, and pieced top—so that it is easy to work with and stays in place while you quilt (this avoids puckering or weird uneven sections of the quilt).

2 There are multiple ways of basting—using pins, glue, stitches—it all depends on what you're comfortable with and what you prefer. I have used many different methods depending on the project and how I'm going to quilt it. Most often, if I am going to machine quilt it myself, I will pin baste. This has given me good results.

3 My favorite tutorial for basting using a table and safety pins is by Carolyn Friedlander and can be found on YouTube under her "Ray Quilt Along 4: Baste and Quilt" tutorial series. I've found this method is great if I don't have a floor to spread out the entire quilt and saves my knees as I can sit and not crawl around the floor pinning my quilt!

Quilt.

1 Often quilt patterns will say something like "quilt as desired" and leave it at that. But that's not great if you've never done this before! There are many options for finishing your quilt:

2 Use your regular sewing machine to quilt—just lengthen your stitch a bit and go a bit slower. A walking foot/even feed foot/quilting foot is a great tool to assist if you have it! Practice on a little sample quilt sandwich to see if you like how your stitches look and to get a feel for how to feed the quilt through your machine.

3 Hand quilting is a great option if you want to slow down and do some hand work. There are lots of tutorials out there for multiple methods of hand quilting. My favorite method is a big stitch method that is a little more modern and less fussy.

4 Tie your quilt! You can absolutely use a tying method to finish your quilt and this is a nice (and relatively quick!) method that makes the quilt very snuggly.

5 Have someone else quilt it! This can be a little pricy, but there are people who quilt and finish quilts if this step gets you stuck.

6 For this project, I did a simple grid quilting design, using straight lines along the seams, using the foot width on my walking foot to guide my stitching lines. This is probably the easiest way to quilt and looks great with all the straight seam lines. I added in a few extra lines and some hand stitching around the center squares to highlight the magenta.

7 Take your time, start slowly, and enjoy the quilting step!

Bind.

1 Now that your quilt is quilted, we need to finish the edges.

2 From your contrast fabric cut six strips 2.5 inches (6.5 cm) wide.

3 Piece strips, end to end, with a diagonal seam, sewing RST. (Q)

4 Trim the excess fabric on the ends. You should now have one very long strip.

5 Using the iron, press the strip in half (seam allowance to the inside). You now have ready-to-use binding. (R)

6 Attach binding to quilt in preferred method. There are many ways to go about doing this. I machine stitch my binding to the front edges of my quilt (S), wrap the binding around to the back and stitch it down by hand. (T) Another popular method is to machine stitch the binding to the back, wrap the binding around to the front of the quilt, and then machine stitch the binding in place, right along the edge of the binding. Again, do what is most comfortable for you! Lots and lots of tutorials exist out there for binding a quilt.

7 Your quilt is done! I always wash my quilts after I finish binding—it fluffs them up, gives them a little crinkle, gets rid of any dust or dirt that found its way on the quilt while I was making it . . . and there's nothing better than pulling a warm quilt out of the dryer!

Robert J. Bosscher is a multiple award-winning quilter and artist. While his creative endeavors have included ceramics, painting, and other mediums, his current passion lies in textile art—specifically quilting. Interested in ideas of transparency as a metaphor and the layers of interpersonal relationships—and influenced by a profound love of color—Robert makes work that is often recognized for its color play and use of neon elements and layered fabrics. Robert's work has been shown internationally in both quilt-specific venues and fine art galleries and museums. Influences in his work extend beyond the quilting world, and include the art of Mark Rothko, Anni and Josef Albers, Felix Gonzalez Torres, and Shoji Hamada, to name a few. Robert has lectured at international quilt shows and continues to work to bridge the gap between traditional craft spaces and the art world, using his unique perspective, informed by his study of art history, to do so. Additionally, Robert has more than ten years of experience teaching, loves helping new makers explore their own creative process, and finds particular joy encouraging students in their exploration of color. His work can be found at rjbosscher.com and on Instagram at @rjbosscher.

CREATED BY

Jen Duffin

YELLOW: Wrapped Fiber Knot

"If you'd like to try your hand at fiber art but don't know where to start, may I suggest fiber emballage? This practice of wrapping one fiber around another has been around for ages, and is often used to create decorative fiber objects for the home. Fiber emballage is simple and easy to pick up, making it the ideal craft for a burgeoning fiber artist. It is also a great way to make use of odds and ends of materials you might have around from other projects."

Fiber emballage, a weaving-adjacent technique, involves the wrapping of fibers (yarn or strips of cloth) around a form or structure (rope, a wooden shape, or another base). *Emballage* is the French word for wrap. The renowned fiber artist Sheila Hicks is credited with creating the technique, and she used it often in works both large and small.

A great way to use up scrap yarn, fiber emballage is also extremely versatile. You can make small wearable pieces like necklaces and bracelets, medium-sized wall hangings, or enormous dimensional works. You can create things in the round or freeform in shape. Practitioners can also incorporate a variety of weaving techniques, as well as knotting, to add complexity and different textures to the fiber emballage works they make.

Conversely, some makers create long lengths of fiber emballage rope which they then use, in turn, as a material in weavings or macrame, making multi-layered, multi-technique creations.

MATERIALS

- 100 feet (30.5 m) of 3 mm cotton string in mustard
- A selection of yellow yarns in various tones, weights, and textures: about 30 feet (9 m) of 7-9 different yarns—approximately 270 feet (82 m) total.
- Measuring tape
- Fabric shears
- Metal yarn needle
- Needle nose pliers (optional)
- Embroidery snips (optional)

INSTRUCTIONS

1 Take the 3 mm cotton string and measure out a length of 75 inches (2 m). Cut, and repeat fifteen times, or until your bundle of string is about 1 inch (2.5 cm) in diameter. Lay the string down on a table and make sure the ends match up.

2 Measure an 8-inch (20 cm) section starting from the ends of the cut string—this will be our tassel at the end so we will NOT wrap this section. The cut ends should face right and the rest of the bundle of string can lay to the left. (A)

3 Take your first yarn choice and lay down a 2-inch (5 cm) tail on top of your string at the 8-inch (20 cm) mark. Taking the yarn bundle in your right hand and holding the yarn tail down with your left hand, wrap the yarn over and around the string. Your wrap should be firm and snug, but you don't need to pull it super tight! This might feel tricky at first as there is nothing holding the string together, but once you get a few wraps in it should feel easier. (B, C, D)

4 Continue wrapping moving towards the left. You want your wraps to butt up against each other. Check every few wraps to make sure that you haven't left gaps—if you have, just gently push the yarn down into place. Continue wrapping until you've covered about 4 inches (10 cm) of string.

TIP: I work right to left because I am right handed; but if it is more comfortable for you, feel free to reverse the direction and wrap left to right.

5 Once you've covered 4 inches (10 cm) of string, we are going to add a second layer. Begin wrapping on top of your first layer of emballage by wrapping left to right. Continue until the section is completely covered. Because you have two layers done, you shouldn't see the string underneath at all. (E)

A

B

C

D

E

6 Cut your yarn from the bundle. (F) Thread your yarn needle with the end of the yarn, and then sew it up underneath your wrapping. Poke the needle out in between two pieces of yarn, and trim flush with the wrapping. (G, H, I) If there is any little bit left, just use the end of your needle to hide it between the yarn wraps. Once finished, you should only see your wrapped section and no cut ends.

7 You've wrapped your first section—wonderful! Now continue on in the same fashion with your other colors of yarn until you get to the end of the string leaving the 8-inch (20 cm) section at the other end for the tassel. (J, K) You can change the size of the sections (they do not all need to be uniform), and repeat yarn colors if desired. You can create a bit of a pattern—repeating colors in sequence if you want. It's totally up to you!

F

G

H

I

J

K

8 Once your string is fully wrapped, it's time to tie it into a knot! The knot we will be tying is called a double coin knot.

- Lay your wrapped string down on a table. Make a loop to the right. (L)
- Make a second loop perpendicular to the first one. (M, N)
- Pass the end under, over, and under the loops (like you are weaving!) (O)
- Pull both ends gently to tighten and to shape the knot evenly. (P)

Voila! You now have a fiber wrapped double coin knot.

L

M

N

O

P

9 You can sew a piece of yarn or string up through the top of the center and back down (knot it and then hide the knot in the wrapping)—this will allow you to hang your knot on the wall. (Q) Taking your fabric shears, you can also trim the tassels to any length you like. (R) Keep them string-like, or you can brush them out for a fluffy effect!

Jen Duffin/Nova Mercury Design is a fiber artist and teacher. Jen has been creating fiber art full-time since 2016, specializing in frame loom weaving. She has taught many sold-out workshops in both Canada and the United States, as well as to international students online. She was selected as a finalist for the 2019 Etsy Awards for her signature rainbow art, and she took home the Canadian People's choice award. She has created a number of e-courses on weaving and recently published her first book *The Joy of Weaving, Modern Frame Loom Projects for Beginners* in 2024. Jen loves creating art that brings joy to people's lives and homes, and to inspire a love of creating in others. She believes in handmade, quality, and small business. She lives with her partner, two children, and dog in Montreal, Canada. Follow her work on Instagram at @novamercury or at www.novamercury.com.

LIME GREEN: Embroidered Fabric Foliage

CREATED BY

Robert Mahar

"What now seems like ages ago, I worked as an art appraiser, studying and cataloging the artwork of others. During that time, I developed a love for both qualitative and quantitative data, which, in turn, led me to a deep appreciation for scientific illustrations. Over time, this fascination evolved into an artistic practice that blends archival imagery with textile techniques. In my embroidery work, I've often used vintage botanical illustrations—printing them on fabric and embellishing them with embroidery. More recently, I've expanded my use of vintage source material beyond two-dimensional illustrations to include three-dimensional representations, inspired by work such as the Blaschka Glass Models of Plants at Harvard. These historical references serve as a springboard for my own three-dimensional recreations of natural specimens in fabric. My interpretations are not intended to be scientifically accurate; rather, they highlight the textiles themselves, celebrating their textures, colors, and construction. They also subtly reference traditional scientific display methods, such as the flat-lay and shadow-box, balancing their scientific influences with an appreciation for decorative objects.

There are a few aspects of this project that I particularly adore. I love that I can create a template from an actual leaf, capturing its organic imperfections rather than a stylized, coloring-book shape. The use of yarn-dyed linen cotton fabric, with its woven texture and subtle color variations, further enhances the natural aesthetic. Wrapping the stems with embroidery floss adds a gentle sheen, and the variegated versions introduce soft tonal shifts. Because the floss is thin, it avoids the bulk of materials like jute, resulting in a well-proportioned stem. Embroidery plays an elegant yet understated role in this work—while not the focal point, it adds delicate texture and visual interest. Through this process, I aim to bridge the worlds of scientific study and textile art, transforming archival imagery into tactile, contemporary objects."

Embroidery—using a needle and thread to decorate a piece of fabric—is a practice that has been around since the dawn of needles, thread, and clothing. Fossilized clothing from 30,000 BCE shows evidence of embroidery! It is a vast practice, touching on almost every culture worldwide. Besides illuminating clothing, religious items, royal garments, and household goods (pillows, blankets, tea towels, etc.), embroidery styles, patterns, and techniques can also give clues to culture, status, and even document important dates and historical events.

The tools of embroidery are easily procurable and endlessly variable. There are literally thousands of stitch types. There are patterns that depict the cutest kittens, recreations of internal organs, and cross-stitch using profanity. Traditional embroidery floss (the thread used) comes in thousands of colors, in a variety of materials from silk to cotton to linen, and there are even companies now that make bespoke hand-dyed skeins. Embroidery can be done on almost any kind of fabric. Thus by mixing and matching, nearly infinite results are possible.

Embroidery is a practice that really does straddle the line between what is art and what is craft. It has oscillated back and forth over the centuries and in our present moment is having something of a revival. No longer relegated to a grandmotherly or Victorian girl tradition, embroidery is used by many as a mixed media embellishment. It is frequently employed as something akin to an act of drawing, rather than a declaration of hand skills.

MATERIALS

- Leaf template
- Light- to medium-weight fabric: some to create leaves and some to create background if you are framing (see resources, below)
- Fabric iron
- Sharp scissors
- Heat erasable marker (see resources, below)
- Paper- or fabric-wrapped floral wire, 26 gauge or similar
- Tacky glue (see resources, below)
- Small flat head paint brush
- 6-strand embroidery floss or perle/ pearl cotton (consider a variegated floss that creates wonderful hue variations)
- Embroidery needle
- Ready-made shadow box (optional)
- Strong double-sided tape (optional; see resources, below)

RESOURCES

- Suggested fabric: Essex linen cotton fabric by Robert Kaufman https://www.robertkaufman.com/ fabrics/essex/
- Heat transfer pen: Frixion Fineliner erasable marker pens by Pilot https://pilotpen.us/ Product?0=41&1=46&cid=100154
- Glue: Aleene's Original Tacky Glue https://aleenes.com/collections/ original-tacky-glue
- Double sided tape: iCraft https://www.thermoweb.com/ products/icraft-supertape-adhesive-roll-br-1-4-in-x-6yd

INSTRUCTIONS

1. Begin by creating a template for your foliage. Leaf shapes can be drawn from memory or imagination, or line drawings can easily be found online. My preferred method is to collect fallen leaves, press them between the pages of an old heavy book and then photocopy the flattened and dried results onto cardstock. (A) Using scissors, trim around the photocopied image—giving yourself permission to simplify details or alter shapes. One alteration that should be included for all templates is the creation of a triangle shape where the base of the leaf meets the stem. This triangle shape will allow you to more seamlessly connect the fabric foliage to its wire stem.

2. Select a light- to medium-weight fabric from which to create your leaves. Quilt-weight cotton fabric is readily available in a wide range of patterns and solid colors. The pictured samples were created using a linen-cotton blend fabric. Know that different patterns and colors can be used for the front and backside of each leaf. Press your chosen fabric with a hot iron and then cut two pieces roughly 1 inch (2.5 cm) larger than your cardstock template. (B)

3. Using a heat erasable marker, trace your cardstock template onto one piece, aligning the bottom of the triangle shape with one edge of the fabric. If you're using a printed textile, be certain to trace the template on the back or "wrong side" of the fabric. Within the traced template shape, draw a line to represent the primary leaf vein down its center. Begin the line roughly 0.5 to 1 inch (1.5 to 2.5 cm) below the tip of the leaf and extend it down through the center of the triangle shape where the leaf stem would be positioned. Next draw one to three pairs of secondary veins that branch off from the primary vein. (C)

4. The drawn vein lines will be used as guides to create a wired interior structure for the fabric leaf and to create its stem. Lightweight floral wire, 26 gauge or similar, is available wrapped in paper or fabric which allows it to most easily be adhered to the leaf fabric. Cut a piece of floral wire that extends the length of your primary leaf vein plus twice the length of your desired stem. (For example, if your primary leaf vein is 3 inches / 7.5 cm and you want to create a 3-inch / 7.5 cm stem, you would need a 9-inch / 23 cm piece of floral wire.) Position the cut piece of floral wire over the drawn primary vein and then fold the stem end in half—creating a double thickness of floral wire for the stem. Then cut a separate piece of floral wire for each pair of secondary veins. (D) Following the drawn secondary vein lines, tightly twist each corresponding piece of floral wire once around the primary vein wire. Set the wired interior structure aside.

A
B
C
D

E
F
G
H
I
J
K
L
M

5 Place the piece of fabric with the traced template and drawn veins on top of a piece of cardboard. Dispense of a bead of tacky glue along the outline of the traced template and loosely fill the interior of the shape. (E) Using a flat head paint brush, quickly work to spread the glue into a thin even layer on the fabric, extending at least 0.5 inch (1.5 cm) beyond the drawn leaf outline. (F) Place the wired veining over drawn vein lines and press into the glue. Dispense a thin bead of tacky glue over the wire and use the paintbrush to make certain it is evenly covered. (G) Position the second piece of fabric on top, aligning the bottom/stem edge and smooth to assure adhesion. Finally, gently run the handle end of the paintbrush along the edges of the wired interior structure to make the leaf veining more pronounced. (H) Set aside for at least 10 minutes, allowing the glue to set up.

6 Position the paper template on top of the wired fabric, aligning it so that the exposed wire stem extends down the center of the triangle form. Press down gently on the paper template to feel the wired structure underneath, adjusting the position of the template to the leaf veining as accurately as possible. Once in place, use a heat erasable marker to outline the template. (I) Cut along the traced lines with scissors. Trim the triangular shape, leaving about ⅛ inch (3 mm) of fabric on either side of the stem. (J)

7 Select a color of 6-strand embroidery floss and cut a 24-inch (61 cm) piece to wrap the wire stem. (K) Tie one end of the embroidery floss to the bent crook of the wire stem, leaving a short 1-inch (2.5 cm) tail. (L) Tightly wrap the embroidery floss around the wire six times—covering what will be the very end of the leaf stem. Bend the wire stem back on itself and continue wrapping both pieces of wire together, disguising the knot tail as you wrap. (M) Slowly wrap your way up the stem towards the leaf, eventually wrapping and disguising the fabric (that was once part of the triangle shape) at the top of the stem. (N) When you reach the very top of the stem, where it abuts the leaf, tightly double knot the embroidery floss. Dab the knot with a small amount of tacky glue and set aside to fully dry and then trim the tail end of the embroidery floss knot. (O) Gently run a warm iron along the edges of the leaf to remove any ink marks. (P)

8 If you'd like to mount in a shadow box, make sure you have strong double-sided tape. Remove the back panel of the shadow box and use it as a template to cut a piece of fabric measuring 2 inches (5 cm) larger on each side. (Q) Use a ruler and a heat erasable marker to draw a series of parallel lines on the fabric. Use three strands of 6-strand embroidery floss to embroider a series of running stitch lines along the drawn guidelines to create a subtly textured background. (R) To make this a running stitch, simply thread an embroidery needle and pass it in and out of the fabric at regular intervals, creating a dashed line of stitches. Wrap the stitched fabric pieces around and adhere to the back of the back panels using the double-sided tape. Gently run a warm iron along the edges of the leaf to remove any ink marks. Reinstall the panels in the shadow boxes and bend the leaves into lifelike positions. Glue them in place using tacky glue and then set aside to dry overnight. (S)

Q

R

S

Robert Mahar is a California-based artist and educator whose work explores the intersection of contemporary aesthetics and historical craft traditions. While a multidisciplinary maker, he is best known for his textile work, which combines vintage imagery with intricate embroidery. In 2005, as handcraft and e-commerce were beginning to converge, Robert launched Mahar Drygoods, a beloved artisan collaborative (now closed) that curated handcrafted goods for children. His passion for championing independent makers led him to become an early adopter of video content, partnering with digital entertainment companies and online learning platforms to create an extensive catalog of tutorials and full-length classes.

Robert was a contestant—and later an associate producer—on NBC's crafting competition show *Making It* with Amy Poehler and Nick Offerman. For the past two decades, he has collaborated with small businesses, cultural institutions, and corporate partners across the United States to develop hands-on workshops tailored to their communities. From fabric embroidery to paper marbling, his creative programming is meticulously researched and uniquely site-specific. Discover more about Robert, explore his video tutorial archive, and browse his collection of embroidered samplers at robert-mahar.com and on Instagram at @robert_mahar.

GREEN: Ombre Cookie Trees

CREATED BY

Crystal Bodven

"My inspiration for this project was born of both my home in the Pacific Northwest and the holidays. Evergreen trees grow everywhere in Washington State. Whenever I travel and then come back home to Seattle, I see the evergreens and know that I am home. As for the holidays—like many hobby bakers, I always found decorating cookies during the holiday season to be a fun activity that brings joy and fills me with nostalgia and memories of childhood. One of the first cookies I ever learned to decorate was a festive holiday tree with a garland and sprinkles. Now, the holidays are a huge part of my business and creating cookies for those special moments in people's lives is one of the biggest joys in my life.

Throughout my life, art and crafts have been a big part of my identity. Being able to create something from nothing with my hands was always very fulfilling. When I found my passion for baking, I started to understand that my language was food; and I wanted to communicate through the art of baking. Decorating cookies gave me the ability to express my love for art through combining painting, sculpting, airbrushing, and creating textures, all onto an edible canvas."

Who doesn't love a good cookie? The first cookies apparently were created in seventh century Persia, perhaps as a means to preserve the staples of nuts, grains, and dates. The bite-sized treats became essential for travelers and soldiers as they were easy to carry. Trade routes spread the deliciousness to Europe, and the word *cookie* evolved from the Dutch word *koekje* meaning "small cake." In England, biscuits were invented. Twice baked, the hard, dry cookies could be stored for a very long time, including during long sea voyages, which was how they eventually made it to the Americas.

Along the way, people began using all kinds of ingredients—honey, chocolate, molasses, a lot of butter—to change the consistency and flavors of their cookies. Cookies began to be associated with holidays and special occasions, but also to be seen as a lovely, decadent everyday treat. While there are so many manufactured cookies available in markets today, there has also been a turn towards the charm and creativity of making your own cookies.

The shape of certain cookies can reflect a visual theme, but these days cookies often serve as a canvas for incredibly creative icing techniques. There are cookies to mark special dates like births or weddings, or cookies to express love of anything at all (plants, animals, cookie monsters). Icing has become like painting—allowing bakers to use time-honored art techniques to generate interesting textures, color palettes, etc. You can now eat a tiny masterpiece—both in how it looks and how it tastes!

MATERIALS

- Sugar cookies (any cookie recipe that has limited spreading after baking, like gingerbread cookies)
- Tree-shaped cookie cutters (see resources, below)
- Royal icing (any recipe will work; see resources, below)
- Green gel food coloring (water-based dyes will make the icing runny)
- Tipless pastry piping bags
- Bag clips or rubber bands (optional)
- Any offset palette knife, butter knife, or metal clay tool
- Scissors

RESOURCES

- Tree-shaped cookie cutters: https://www.annclark.com/
- Genie's Dream Meringue Powder (my favorite for making Royal icing): https://geniesproducts.com/

TIPS

- **Icing Consistency:** Icing should be at stiff peaks. If the icing is too runny, you can add powdered sugar a little at a time and mix until desired consistency. To test, you can use a palette knife, spatula, or spoon and swipe it. If the icing holds its shape, it is ready to pipe.
  Color the Icing as you want; you can make one color or several. (A)
- **Using Piping Bags:** Fill the piping bag(s) with icing no more than halfway. Push the icing down towards the end of the tip. You can use bag clips or rubber bands or tie a knot to seal the pastry bag so the icing doesn't come out while squeezing. Seam side up, take your scissors and cut a little bit of the tip. Start small because you can always make it bigger.

INSTRUCTIONS

1. Pipe a row of icing dots on a cookie. The bigger the dots, the more icing you have to work with to smoosh the icing and create a groove. Green was the choice here, but we can imagine these in any color; do a solid row of one color or mix them up! (B)
2. Turn the cookie so the point of the tree is in the direction where you will guide your offset palette knife (or your preferred tool). Hold your tool over one of the first dots, leaving one-third of it exposed and press into the dot gradually towards the top point of the tree creating a groove. Repeat the process with the rest of the dots in the row. The part you smush down can extend as far as you'd like. Do not worry if they are all the same length as they will get covered by your next row. (If you should choose to use various colored dots and want to keep the colors clean, wipe the tool with a wet paper towel after the swipe of each colored dot.) (C, D)

A

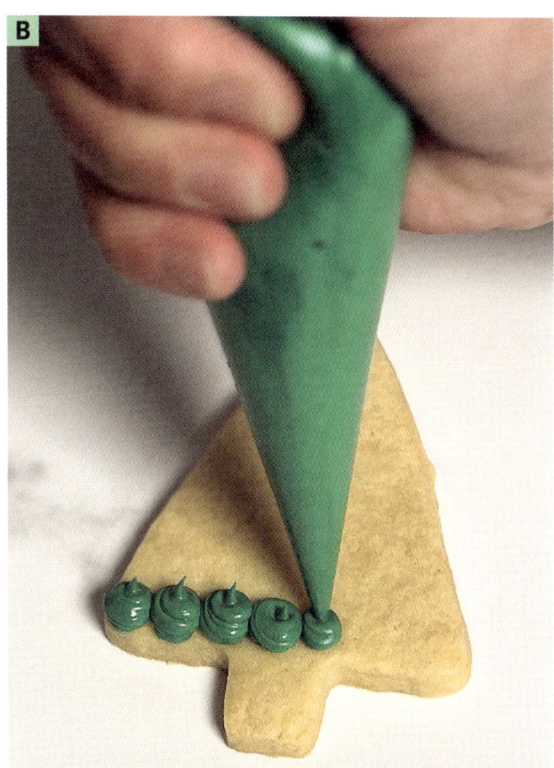
B

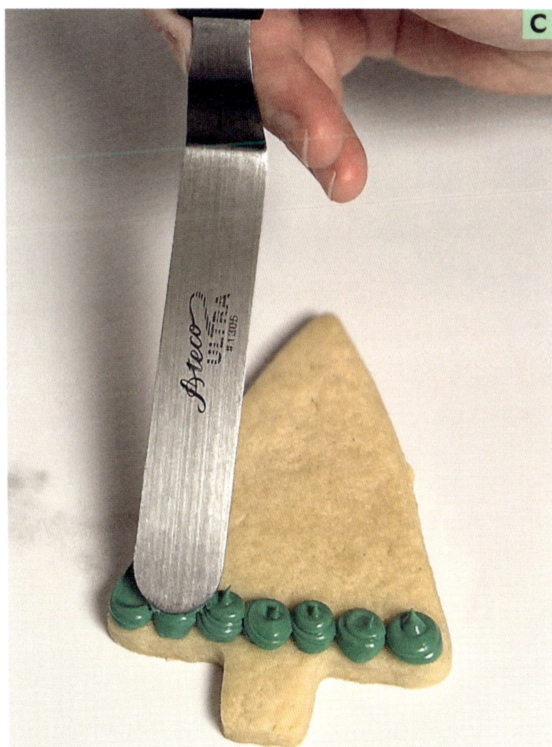
C
Ateco
ULTRA
#1305

D

3. Start on the next row where'd you like. You can work evenly in rows or more organically. If you want very even rows, draw out lines ahead of time where you would like the layers of icing to go. Repeat making dots and smushing them in rows until you get to the row before tip of your cookie. (E, F)

4. When you reach the last layer for the top of the tree, pipe one to three dots and aim the smoosh towards the tip. On that last dot, scrape excess icing off on the sides. (G)

5. "Spruce it up!" (suggested decorations)

   - Add a trunk by painting, scraping, or piping brown icing
   - Add sprinkles or edible glitter (apply when the icing is still wet)
   - Add little details like snow, mushrooms, woodland creatures, or birds
   - Pipe a garland or string of lights

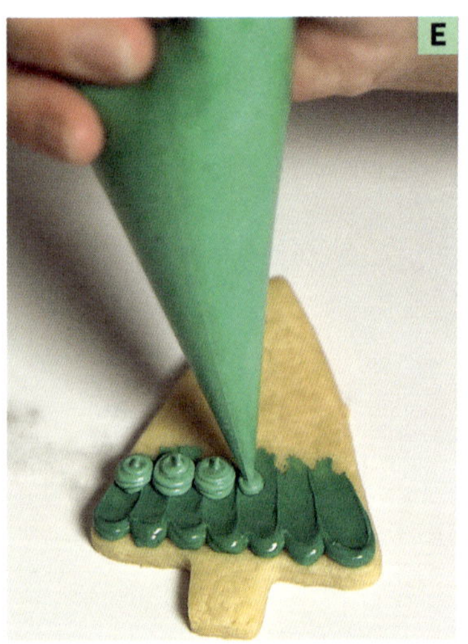
E

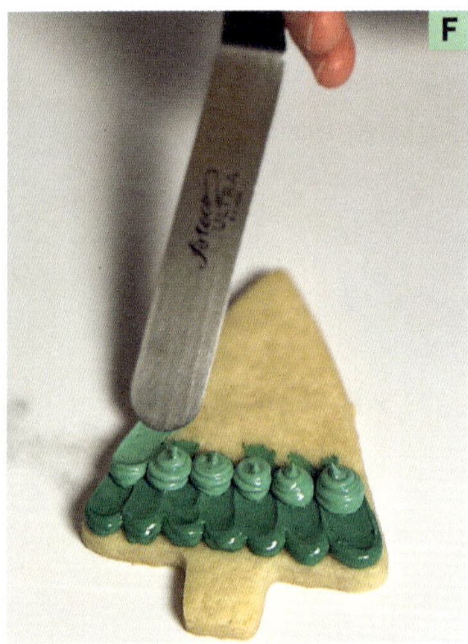
F

G

Crystal Bodven has always been creative, teaching herself how to bake, knit, sew, paint, and make jewelry. She moved to the Seattle area shortly after high school to enroll in the Pastry and Baking Program at South Seattle College. After graduating, she worked various jobs in dessert production—pie maker, cake decorator, pastry assistant—and then landed her dream job as a Chocolatier at Theo Chocolate.

During the upheavals and uncertainty of the Covid pandemic, Crystal created a new Instagram account in the middle of the night. It was called Crystallized Cookies and, just months after opening the account, she left her job to start her cookier journey. By the end of that year, Crystallized Cookies was officially a business! Since opening her business, Crystal has been specializing in custom orders for parties, events, corporations, pop-ups, and markets that showcase her skill and attention to detail. Once a year, Crystal attends CookieCon (Yes, there is a cookie convention!) to learn new skills and connect with other cookiers. She is excited to spread joy one cookie at a time. Her Instagram and Facebook are @CrystallizedCookies and you can visit her site at CrystallizedCookies.com

DARK GREEN: Knitted Cowl

CREATED BY

Dana Williams Johnson

"Green is one of my favorite colors. When I think of dark green, I think of rich and dark and cozy things. It always makes me think of winter and evergreen trees and the smell of pine, so I thought it would only be right to make a dark green cowl. Something warm to keep the wind off my neck on the colder days. My favorite kind of cowl to knit is one with colorwork. I find that knitting in the round, and grafting the ends together using Kitchener stitch, gives a hand-knit cowl a very clean look. Plus, it makes it doubly warm and cozy, which is what you really want on a cold and windy day.

When it comes to knitting, colorwork is one of my favorite techniques. Bringing in colors and patterns, seeing the shapes emerge, makes it fun to knit. Since I would pair this cowl with a coat, I wanted to keep the pattern simple but still add a bit of visual interest. I went with a color-shifting yarn that had darker and subtler colors so that it didn't overpower the dark green main color. I wanted it to enhance the project and not take it over. The cowl can also be easily modified. You can make it longer for a cowl that can wrap around your neck twice, or cast on fewer stitches to make a smaller version for a child (or even your dog)."

The word knitting comes from the word knot. The first knitted socks which were discovered in Egypt were made in the third through fifth centuries. The technique spread across Europe, with some countries—particularly Scandinavian ones—figuring out how to knit complex patterns and designs. Knitting is a process that uses two often pointed needles to loop yarn to create an interconnected fabric. Knitting differs from weaving which uses a loom and an over-under threading technique, and from crochet which uses a single hooked needle to generate loops.

In 1589, an industrial knitting machine was invented by William Lee, an English clergyman. Up to that point many people knitted sweaters, socks, and other garments. Some held great importance, such as the Fair Isle fisherman sweaters in Scotland. Each family had its own design so that men could be identified if lost at sea. The wool was also protective—the oils in the wool helped keep the fishermen warm and dry. Industrial knitting slowly pushed knitting out of daily life but it has continually made a resurgence. This has sometimes happened in times of need, such as during the World Wars when people were encouraged to knit hats and other garments for soldiers, and also to take apart and remake their own sweaters since material was short in supply.

The internet actually has helped spur a knitting revival in our own time. People relish sharing techniques and patterns with one another online. And as with many other "handicrafts," contemporary folks have found knitting to be relaxing, enjoyable, and good for the maker's mental health.

MATERIALS

- Worsted weight yarn
  - Main color (MC): 300 yards (274 m) (see resources, below)
  - Contrasting color (CC): 200 yards (183 m) (see resources, below)
- Needles: US #8/5.00 mm – 16-inch (40.5 cm) circulars (two pairs needed)
- Crochet hook in comparable size for provisional cast on
- One stitch marker
- Waste yarn for provisional cast on
- Gauge: sixteen stitches by twenty-eight rows per 4-inch (10 cm) square worked in Stockinette stitch

RESOURCES

- Porter Wool Co Organic Merino Worsted in Huntress - 100% wool; 218 yards per 100g color Huntress https://porterwoolco.com/
- Spincycle Dream State - 100% wool; 150 yards in Birds of a Feather https://spincycleyarns.com/

TIP

This cowl starts with a provisional cast on and is worked in the round until the preferred length is achieved. Once length has been achieved, the provisional cast on is removed and the two ends of the cowl are grafted together seamlessly using Kitchener stitch. You can make the cowl as long as you would like but note that it will increase the yardage of yarn you will need.

CHART

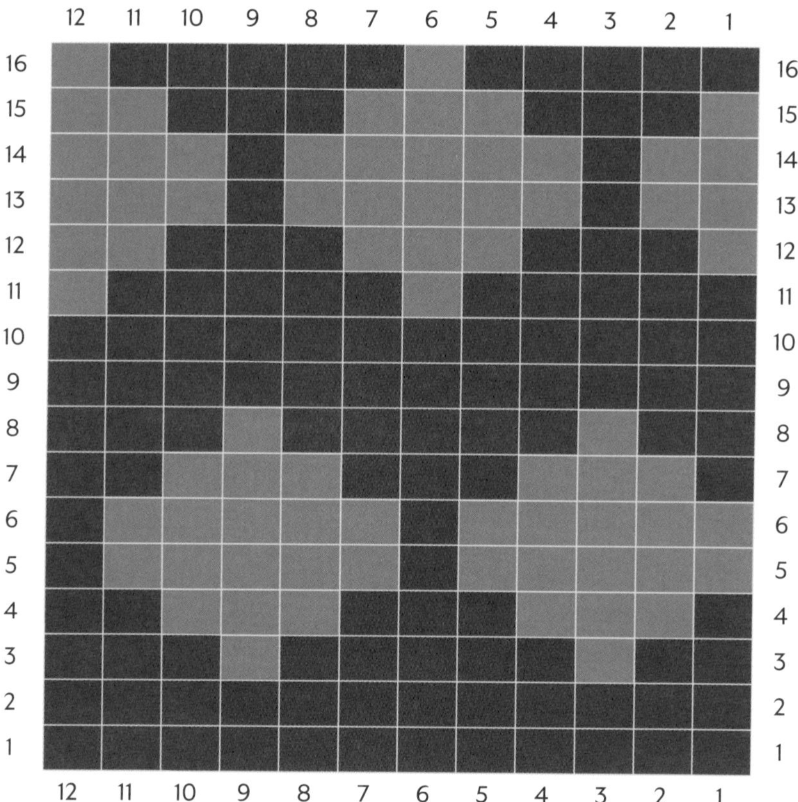

INSTRUCTIONS

1. Provisionally cast on eighty four stitches with scrap yarn (I used red). (A)
2. Using MC, place your beginning of round marker and join in the round being careful not to twist the stitches.
3. Work rows one through sixteen of the colorwork chart until the cowl reaches 26 inches (66 cm) or your preferred length for a longer cowl. (B)
4. Cut CC once the length has been reached. (C)

A

B

C

5 Continue using MC, remove the provisional cast on and place live stitches on your needle.

6 Using the Kitchener stitch, join the provisional cast on with the live stitches to create a circular tube for your cowl. (D)

7 Finishing: Weave in your grafted end, block, and wear! (E)

Dana Williams-Johnson is an academic, avid reader, dog mom, and obsessed knitter. As a professor with a doctorate in Communications, Culture, and Media Studies, her work is rooted in feminist studies around social media and online communities. Her love of knitting spills into her research work—she has studied online knitting communities, and Black women who knit were her research subjects. In her free time, she writes for her blog, Yards of Happiness, about her many colorful knitting projects and what brings her joy on a daily basis. She also has a monthly column on Modern Daily Knitting where she shares her favorite sweater patterns and projects for her dogs. Her favorite knitting projects are tiny sweaters for her Chihuahuas, Jellybean and Kiwi, and the occasional sweater request from her husband. Although green is her favorite color, she tries to knit rainbows any chance she gets. You can see more of her work at yardsofhappiness.com, professordwj.com, and moderndailyknitting.com/contributors/dana-williams-johnson.

INDIGO: Bird Paper Cut

CREATED BY

Kanako Abe

"I like creating artwork that goes beyond aesthetics, with the intention of offering a sense of meditation and healing. This design features a swallow flying over waves, always accompanied by a sun or moon watching over her. The background pattern is inspired by Seigaiha*, a traditional Japanese motif symbolizing gentle waves that stretch endlessly—it embodies tranquility and the wish for a peaceful life to continue for eternity, and is regarded as an auspicious pattern. All elements are encompassed within the circle. In Zen philosophy, the circle is a powerful symbol of infinity, representing both the beginning and the end of all things. The circle's continuous, uninterrupted flow—without corners to hinder its movement—reflects the Buddhist teaching of a liberated mind, free from attachment and desire, existing in a state of pure freedom.*

I first tried cutting paper over ten years ago, and it instantly clicked, as I've always enjoyed working with intricate details. The process also felt incredibly meditative, requiring my full focus on the tip of the blade. But what I love most about cut paper art is its simplicity—you're working with just one material, which challenges and sparks creativity. Cut paper art also brings me back to my late grandfather, a truly creative person who could fix anything and craft toys or objects from scraps of wood and random materials. To me, it was like magic—how he could transform ordinary materials into something special. He was the first person to teach me that all you need is creativity. During the pandemic, when everything felt out of control, I began dyeing my paper, intentionally introducing something more organic and unpredictable into my process, and I've learned to embrace whatever result emerges."

Paper cutting dates back to near the invention of paper itself. Paper was created in China in 105 CE, and evidence of paper cut works have been found from the fourth to sixth centuries. Originally paper cuts (*jianzhi*) were created as religious offerings featuring gods and various flora and fauna. As paper became more widely available, red paper (considered lucky) was used to create *jianzhi* for weddings and other celebrations. Paper cuts were soon being used as embroidery templates—as a means to transfer complicated designs onto the fabric to be stitched. The technique spread first to other areas in Asia (in the eighth and ninth centuries), then made its way to Europe (in the thirteenth century), and Turkey (in the sixteenth century).

Paper cuts are often used decoratively for celebrations and religious purposes, mirroring cultural elements in their design. For example, in Mexico *papel picado* banners hang in Día de Muertos altars and in Japan *kirigami*—which combine both origami and cut paper techniques—are popular. Many other cultures also have rich paper cutting traditions: *Scherenschnitt* in Switzerland and Germany, *Wycinanki* in Poland, *Wayang* (also called *wajang* or *wayang kulit*), shadow puppetry in Indonesia, Thailand, Cambodia, Laos, and Malasia, and *Hiddur Mitzvah* in Judaism.

Paper is ubiquitous in our lives today. Anyone with some scissors (or even a willingness to tear strategically!) can create a paper cut. Those who want to invest in some smaller scissors or precision utility knives can work toward creating more complicated and delicate patterns.

MATERIALS

To dye your own indigo paper (optional)

- Washi paper 20lb or less (see resources, page 144) cut into larger than 7-by-7-inch (18 by 18 cm) square
- Prepare multiple sheets, including a few for testing or in case of a mistake
- A plastic utility tub or any container—like a small baking sheet, larger than the paper size
- Another small tub for rinsing the paper (optional)
- Indigo dye kit, or dye of your choice
- Latex gloves
- Pants hangers with clips or clothesline with clips for drying (have as many hangers as the number of sheets you plan to dye)
- If you don't have space for hang-drying and are drying the paper flat, have newspaper available.

- *For cutting paper*
- Cutting mat
- Printer paper or any other you have on hand (20lb paper weight recommended)
- Indigo-dyed paper, larger than 7-by-7 inches (18 by 18 cm)
- Washi tape or masking tape
- Sketching materials (pencil, eraser, drawing compass, and marker) or a drawing app such as Procreate
- Precision knife such as X-ACTO—although I prefer a NT cutter (see resources, page 144)
- Replacement blades
- Pattern—use mine (shown at 100% size on page 145) or draw your own

RESOURCES

- Kozo washi from Awagami Factory, paper weight 45gsm https://awagami.com/collections/fine-art-papers/products/fine-art-paper-pack-15sheets-kozo-thick-45gsm
- Indigo dye kit from Dharma https://www.dharmatrading.com/kits/starter/sets/indigo-dye-kit.html
- NT cutter basic precision knife with resin holder, D-400 (I find it easier than X-ACTO as blades don't snap easily.) https://www.ntcutter.co.jp/en/products/detail/250
- Replacement blades, 30 degrees https://www.ntcutter.co.jp/en/products/detail/52
- Knife & blades also available on Amazon

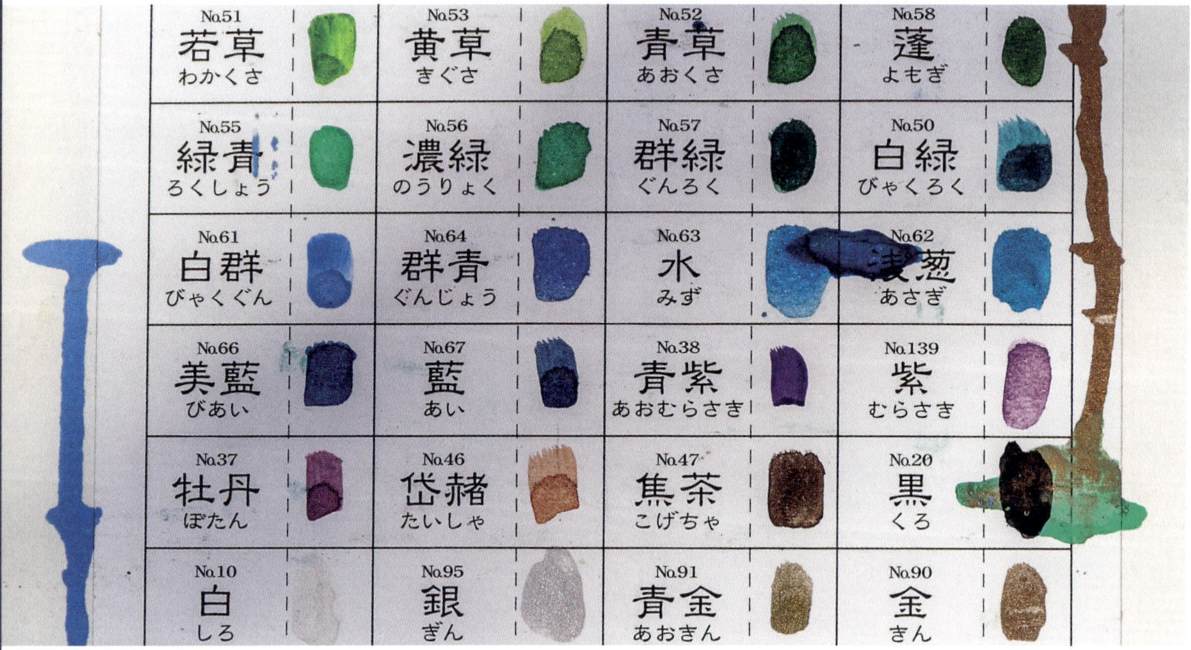

PATTERN

INSTRUCTIONS

For dyeing paper

1 Perform the dyeing in a well-ventilated area. Prepare a small indigo dye bath according to the instructions on the package. Since you're only dyeing small pieces of paper, you'll only need a fraction of the dye. (If you're using the indigo dye kit, about one-quarter of the package should be sufficient.) Create the bath in your small, plastic container or baking sheet. (A)

2 Wear latex gloves to avoid staining your fingers. Use the clips from the hanger to pinch the top of the paper. (B)

3 When dyeing the paper in the dye bath, avoid fully submerging or dipping the paper. Instead, gently place the paper on the surface of the dye to prevent unwanted folds or creases. Start by letting the bottom edge of the paper touch the dye near the edge of the bath, then slowly lower the rest of the paper to lay it flat on the surface. (It's important to do this in one continuous motion, without pausing, as the pigment begins to absorb as soon as the paper makes contact with the dye.) (C)

4 Indigo dye naturally produces a residue that floats on the surface, thus your first few attempts may result in paper with an uneven texture. (D) After few attempts, the paper will have less residue. When the paper first touches the dye, it will appear greenish; but it will soon turn indigo as it oxidizes. (E)

5 Once the paper is dyed, you can gently rinse any residue with tap water. (F) A sink with a shower attachment works well, or you can gently rinse it in another tub filled with clean water. (G) If you are planning to hang-dry, do not remove the paper from the hanger. If air-drying indoors, it's a good idea to cover any surfaces with a plastic sheet and place a towel under the dyed paper to prevent any unwanted stains. Hang the paper or lay it flat on a piece of newspaper to help soak up excess moisture. (H, I) Leave overnight to fully dry.

A
B
C
D
E
F
G
H
I

For cutting paper

1. Create a sketch for your project with pencil on the plain paper. I drew a circle containing a swallow flying over waves, along with a sun/moon. (J) (You can use the pattern provided or create your own design (see page 145). If you scan and print the pattern provided, you can skip to step 3).

2. Trace your sketch with a marker. (K) This step is important, as the clear, defined lines will guide where to cut, blurry pencil lines will be challenging to follow.

3. Cut the paper with the design to slightly smaller than the indigo paper. Lay the indigo-dyed paper flat on a surface, then place the design paper on top. Make sure that both sheets of paper are completely flat, then secure it in place with washi tape or masking tape as shown in the image. Place the paper on a cutting mat. (L)

4. Time to start cutting! Start by cutting the edge of the black line. Do not cut the middle of the lines. There's no set rule for where to begin, but I find it easier to start with the smallest details, as they require the most attention.

5. For this pattern, I recommend starting with the swallow in the center. You will be cutting through both sheets of paper. (M)

6. As you cut, start with the bottoms of your lines first. Follow with the top line to complete the cut. At the start and stop of your lines where they intersect, instead of cutting to a point, extend each line slightly beyond creating a small X. This technique will help create cleaner cuts.

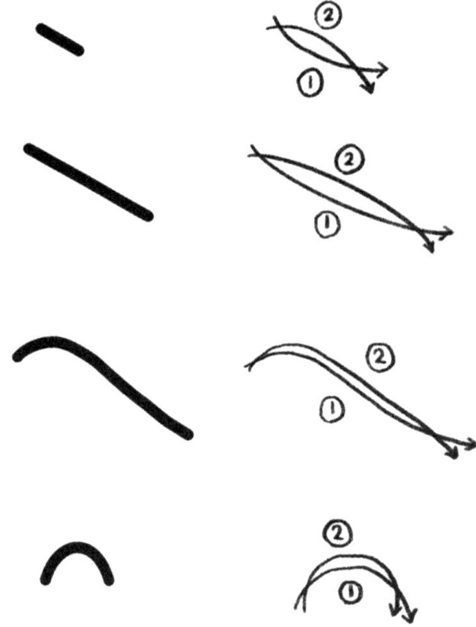

7. After making the cut, gently lift the piece from the sketch using the tip of the blade (N). If you're unsure whether each cut is successful, you can lift the paper and check it from the backside. (O)

8. As you are cutting, feel free to rotate the paper. (P) This will help in areas like the half-circles on the bird's neck.

J
K
L
M
N
O
P

Q
R
S
T
U
V
W
X

9 Once you've finished the most delicate section (in this design, the bird), move on to the background pattern. Keep in mind it's easier to start from the bottom, moving toward the top and also left to right (if you are right-handed). For this pattern, we will divide the cutting into three sections.

10 When cutting the wave pattern, you can either cut section by section, or if you are comfortable, you can cut curvy lines all at once, then move onto cutting the sides to complete the cuts.

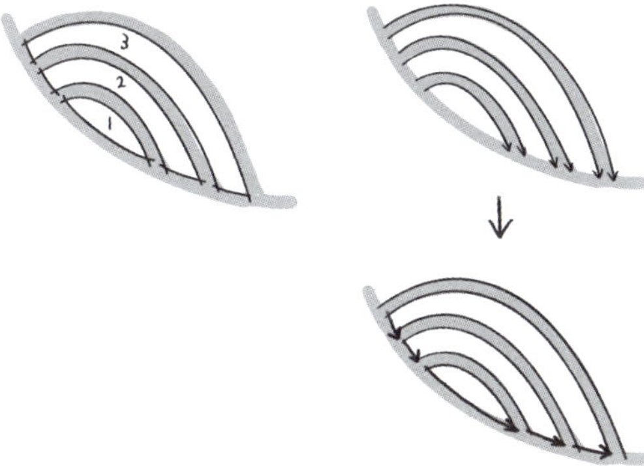

11 Rotate the paper as needed, and change the blade as soon as it starts to feel less sharp. Move from section to section until you have cut all the waves. (Q, R, S, T) Do not cut the outer outline of the large circle until you have finished.

12 Once all the wave patterns are cut, begin cutting the outer outline of the circle. Avoid cutting it all at once, as this could cause the paper to pull and shift. Instead, cut gradually while keeping the tip of the blade in constant contact with the paper. Place your fingertip close to the area you're cutting to ensure the paper stays flat and the upper layer doesn't shift. Rotate the paper as needed. (U)

13 Gently remove the pattern paper on top and the excess paper around the circle. You can use the tip of the blade to carefully lift and separate the pieces, or remove any stray cut pieces. Ta-da! You did it! (V, W, X)

14 When mounting the paper for framing, place small pieces of double-sided tape on the back of the larger sections—in this case, the moon/sun and the swallow's head are ideal. The red squares (Y) indicate suggested areas for the tape. Secure the artwork onto backing paper or a matte for framing. (Z) Glue sticks are not recommended since the paper is delicate and lightweight. The glue may cause wrinkles. NEVER use spray adhesive, as it can damage the artwork immediately, leading to disaster!

Kanako Abe is a *kirie* artist based in Seattle, WA. Specializing in the Japanese art of paper cutting, she meticulously crafts artworks by cutting intricate designs using a precision knife. Kanako elevates her work by hand-dying washi paper, often utilizing indigo, rust, or Japanese sumi ink to create an imperfect texture—representing the delicate balance between the unexpected and control.

Originally from Tochigi Prefecture in Japan, Kanako spent her childhood immersed in the natural beauty of the Nasu Highlands. She moved to California as an international student, graduating from San Francisco State University with a degree in Theatre Arts. Following a few years working in costume and prop design, she turned to the art of paper cutting, returning to Japan for a year to study *Isekatagami*, a traditional Japanese cut-paper stencil technique used in kimono textile printing. This profoundly influenced her work, helping refine her ability to cut delicate, intricate patterns. Upon her return to the United States, she dedicated herself to developing her technique. Since then, her pieces have been featured in both solo and group exhibitions in San Francisco, Los Angeles, and Portland. You can see more of her work on Instagram at @abemanatee and at kanakoabe.art.

BLUE: Punch Needle Wall Hanging

CREATED BY

Rashida Coleman-Hale

"I was excited to do a punch needle project and knew right away that I wanted it to be a wall hanging. They're such an easy make that could be a wonderful gift or a nice way to show off your new punch needle skills. I designed this floral print for my fabric collection, Salutations. I love how graphic the flowers are in this print, and I couldn't wait to see the design translated to this medium."

Punch needle embroidery—aka rug hooking—is a contemporary technique born out of a desire to create something functional. The origin of the craft itself is historically unclear with various people pointing to examples in ancient Egypt, medieval Europe, Russia, Germany, and Britain.

The first punch needle tool, called "The Griffin," was invented in 1881 and patented by an Ebenezer Ross in Toledo, Ohio. In the late nineteenth century with the Industrial Revolution in full swing, machine-made rugs became all the rage for the upper and middle classes. Some workers in the factories that created these luxury rugs were allowed to take home the wool scraps, about 9 inches (23 cm) long, and use those scraps to create carpets for their own homes. But rug hooking as a practice, particularly in the United States, most likely began earlier. Scraps of yarn and fabric were pushed through a mesh or canvas fabric—often leftover burlap sacks—with a small hook, similar to a crochet hook. This allowed people to make floor coverings of their own.

As with many of the domestic arts, punch needling took on a life of its own—with some women skillfully creating beautiful objects that no longer just sat on the floor but were hung on the walls, or adorned clothing, pillows, etc. It is currently quite easy to find beautiful contemporary examples on any social media platform. As the technique has become elevated in status, more and more people have begun using different sized needles and threads to create all kinds of work—smaller punch needles use thinner threads and can create more detailed designs on things like t-shirts, patches, etc. Punch needle embroidery is easily adapted to explore abstract, pictorial, contemporary, or historical representations in sizes from large to small.

MATERIALS

- Worsted weight yarn
  - Background (cobalt blue): approximately 195 yards (178.5 m) (see resources, below)
  - Petals (light blue): approximately 42 yards (38.5 m) (see resources, below)
  - Stem (navy blue): approximately 38 yards (34.5 m) (see resources, below)
  - Center (pale blue): approximately 3 yards (25 m) (see resources, below)
- Oxford punch Needle #14 Fine Point
- Monk's Cloth
- Four pieces of art canvas stretcher bars—14 inches (35.5 cm) in length (you can buy these easily in art stores—they are sold pre-fab and ready to slip together)
- Hammer or mallet
- Staple gun
- Pencil
- Scissors
- Masking tape
- Craft felt for backing
- PVA glue
- Paint brush
- Template (see page 158)—copy or scan and enlarge by 150%

RESOURCES

Wool of the Andes yarn is available in many brick and mortar as well as online stores. This project uses the colors Arctic, Celestial, Whirlpool, and Peacoat.

TEMPLATE

Copy or scan template, increasing size by 150%, final size should be approximately 8.5 x 8.5 inches (22 x 22 cm)

INSTRUCTIONS

Making the Frame

1 Use the mallet to help assemble frames: the corners should fit together, then hammer them to secure in place without a gap.

2 Staple the joints of the frame to keep the frame assembled. (A)

3 Lay Monk's cloth under the frame and make sure there is at least 2 inches (5 cm) of extra cloth on all sides of the frame. (B)

4 Starting on one side of the frame, staple the Monk's cloth to the frame. Start stapling from the center towards the outer edges. Place staples about ½ inch (1.5 cm) apart. Do not staple the cloth to the corners.

5 Turn so the opposite side of the staples side is facing you. Pull the cloth as taut as possible and staple as before. Make sure to keep the cloth tight without puckering.

6 Staple the third side, again stapling from the center towards the outer edge.

7 Now staple the last side. (C) Remember to pull the cloth as taut as possible as you staple. Press the front of the fabric with your finger to make sure that it is drum tight. (D)

8 Trim any excess fabric.

9 Fold the fabric over on the corners and staple them to secure—there are several methods to do this. I prefer creating a triangle which I staple to the back, but since the work will eventually be taken off the frame, the corners are not super important.

A

B

C

D

Transferring the Image

1 Print and cut out the template. (E) Tape it to the *back* of the monk's cloth.

2 Hold up the frame to a lightbox or a window and trace the lines to the front of the monk's cloth with a pencil. (F)

Threading the Needle

1 Insert the yarn through the eye of the slotted side of the needle.

2 Guide the yarn through the slot and pull to maneuver the yarn into the slot. (G)

3 Pull the yarn back through the eye so that a max of 2 inches (5 cm) is hanging on the end. (H)

Punching

1 Be sure that the opening of the needle is facing the direction that you would like to stitch. I like to start with the smallest shapes and work my way up to the largest in this order: The dot, the stem, the petals, the background.

2 Using the pencil lines as a guide, insert the needle all the way into the Monk's cloth (the base of the wooden handle should touch the cloth when you punch) and then pull it straight up. Be careful not to pull the needle all the way out as it will pull out your stitch. The tip of the needle should glide along the fabric as you make your stitches. Skip two to three mesh holes in the cloth and reinsert the needle into the fabric.

3 Start by stitching the outlines with about six stitches per inch (2.5 cm). Fill in the shapes with about four stitches per inch (2.5 cm). Try to keep your stitches uniform throughout. (I, J, K, L)

4 When you come to a corner and need to change directions, keep the needle down and pivot toward the direction you'd like to go. Alternatively, you can turn the entire frame.

5 Continue filling in the shapes. Once you've made your last stitch, keep the needle in place. Turn the work over and clip the yarn to the same length as the loops. Pull your needle back through to the front side of the wall hanging.

6 Once you've completed punching all of the shapes, clean up the design on the front side. Use an empty punch tool to move loops into their correct position to help define the borders of each shape.

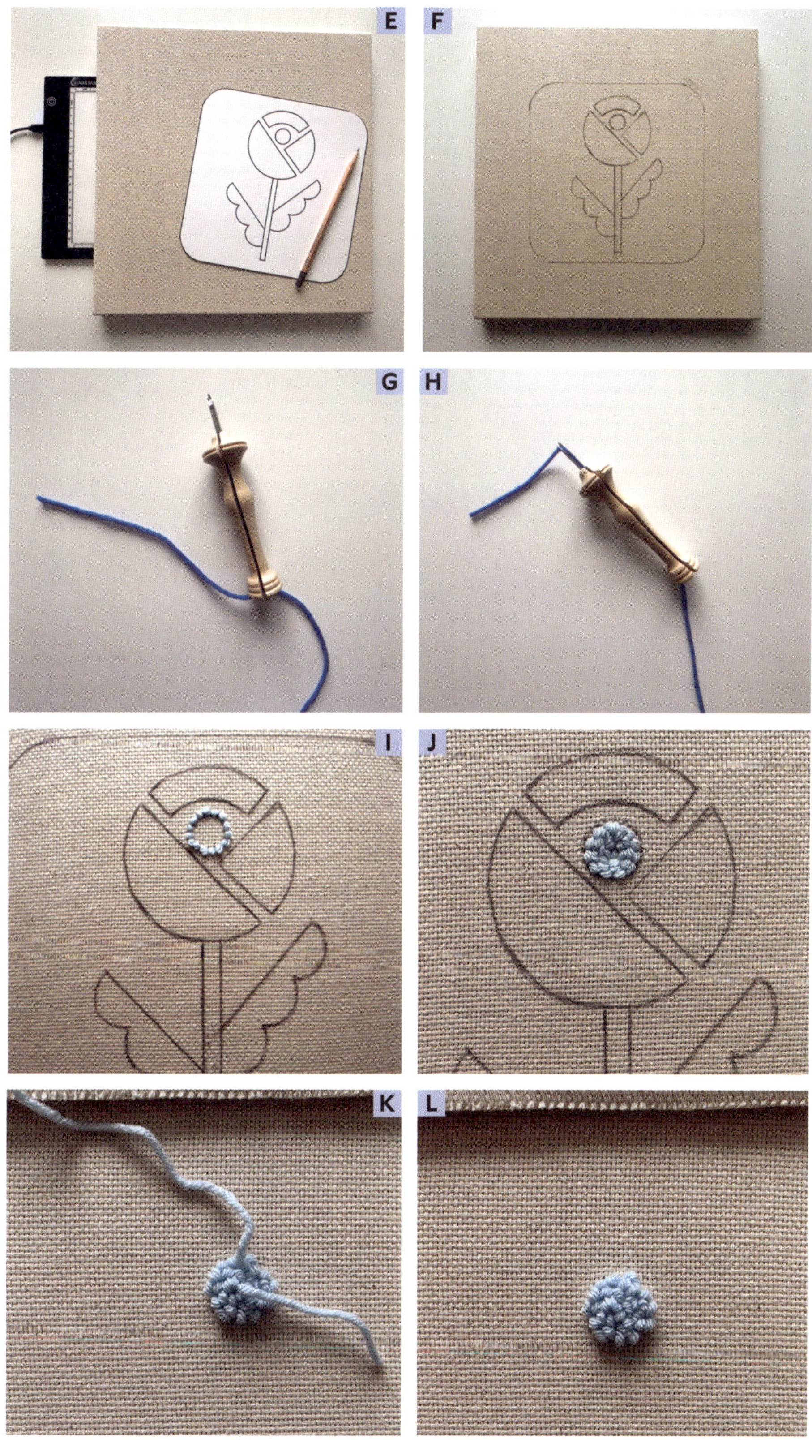
E
F
G
H
I
J
K
L

Finishing

1 Clip any random strands of yarn as necessary, especially on the backside. (L)

2 Cut the felt to the shape of the wall hanging using the template as a guide.

3 Remove the wall hanging from the frame and trim the fabric leaving a 1-inch (2.5 cm) allowance around your design. (M)

4 Fold the edges of the fabric towards the wrong side and tack down with a bit of glue.

5 Brush the back of the hanging with a light coat of glue being careful not to get any glue on the front or the edges. (N) Place the felt on the glue and smooth the lining up the edges. (O)

6 Set aside to dry. If you want to hang your piece on a wall, add a loop of rope, or a more traditional art hanging device on the felt.

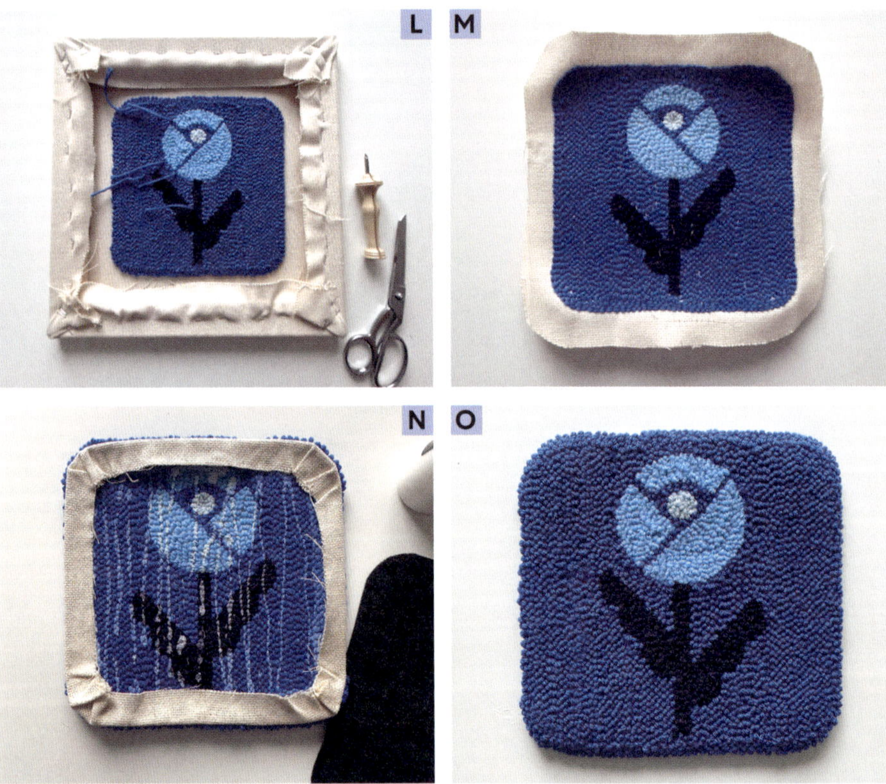

Rashida Coleman-Hale has been drawing ever since she could pick up a pencil and her passions include illustration, textile design, surface pattern design, and fiber arts. Inspired by countless summers in Japan with her fashion model mother, the California-based designer has lived a life brimming with excitement and inspiration. After attending FIT in New York, she ended up trading the fashion world for design, teaching herself Photoshop and Illustrator and dabbling in freelance graphic design, but she can actually credit motherhood for her segue to fabric design.

In the fifteen years since Rashida Coleman-Hale became a fabric designer, she's worked with Cloud9 Fabrics; co-founded Cotton + Steel; and ultimately landed at Ruby Star Society where she has been a designer for over ten years. She has also authored two award-winning sewing how-to books, *I Love Patchwork* and *Zakka Style* and released her third book *Zakka Sewn* in 2025. Her work has been featured at Target, Blue Sky Planners, Maisonette, Petite Plume, *Flow* Magazine, Moda Fabrics, Cloud 9 Fabrics, Renaissance Ribbons, OESD, Meori, Bloom Baby, Winter Water Factory, and Hazel Village. You can follow her creative journey on Instagram @iamrashidacolemanhale or her website www.rashidacolemanhale.com.

PERIWINKLE: Crocheted Religieuse

CREATED BY

Twinkie Chan

"The religieuse *is a classic French pastry, and its shape is meant to resemble a nun in a habit. To make this delicious treat out of real pastry, you begin with two choux buns, filled with luscious crème pâtissière and covered in ganache or icing. Then you join the buns with a dainty, piped buttercream which represents a ruffle or collar. I was first inspired to create a crocheted version of this adorable cream puff tower for an installation in Dallas that I designed to be my dream crocheted bakery. Simple crochet shapes, a few yarny squiggles, and just the right hues can send your imagination to a warm and cheerful room filled with the scent of sugar, butter, and vanilla."*

Many needle arts—knitting, embroidery, weaving—can be historically dated and their origins unearthed. It's a bit trickier with crochet. Did it derive from Chinese needlework? Or from the region around modern-day Turkey/Persia/North Africa where a historical process known as tambouring was something like a cross between embroidery and rug hooking? Historians see evidence of what we know today as crochet turning up in Europe in the early 1800s. Its use of a single needle with a curved hook on the end distinguishes it from knitting which uses two pointy-ended needles. Although it is true that many people cannot tell the difference between the end-result fabrics that the two techniques produce.

Originally, crochet was used to make garments and useful items. Men crocheted fishing nets, game bags, etc. It's speculated that crochet allowed the masses to recreate the expensive lace and decoration that appeared on the clothing of the wealthy. During the Irish Potato Famine of 1845 to 1850, selling crocheted items (that whole households worked on together) helped save many families. In fact, it appears that the earnings from these sales helped fund many Irish immigrations, particularly to the United States, spreading the skills and craft of crochet worldwide.

In the early twentieth century useful but fun decorative items began to be made—hot water bottle and tea cozies, fruity potholders. The portability of the small tools allowed people to take their crochet on the road and make during meetings, waiting for school pickups, at the park, on the bus, and so forth. Of course it wasn't long before crochet made its appearance in the fine art realm. Even the crocheted doily—long imagined to be the decoration on the back of grandma's couch—has been flipped on its head to adorn walls in artistic prominence.

MATERIALS

- Worsted weight yarn
  - Beige: approximately 40 yards (36.5 m) (see resources, below)
  - Light Blue: approximately 30 yards (27.5 m) (see resources, below)
  - Natural: approximately 10 yards (9 m) (see resources, below)
- H/8 5.0 mm crochet hook
- Small amount of polyester stuffing
- Yarn needle
- Stitch marker or a piece of yarn in a contrasting color
- Embellishments like acrylic faux sprinkles or pearls, super fine glitter and brush, hot glue gun for crochet parts, Loctite Super Glue Ultra Gel or Fabri-Tac for small plastic pieces (optional)

RESOURCES

- Cascade 220 in 8412 Pear, 1006 Sky Blue, 8010 Natural from JimmyBeansWool.com

TIPS

- The right side of your work is the side that faces you when you while you crochet. The right side should always be the outside of your project.
- Rnd 1 of the choux buns is the top of the bun.
- The choux buns won't look like perfect spheres. They are designed to look a little squashed or flatter than a perfect sphere, so there's no need to stuff them too firmly.

ABBREVIATIONS IN US TERMS

Ch(s): chain(s)

Inv dec: invisible decrease (Insert hook into front loop only of next st. Insert hook into front loop only of following st. YO and pull through first 2 loops on hook, YO and pull through remaining 2 loops on hook.)

Rnd(s): round(s)

St: stich

Sc: single crochet

Sk: skip

Sl st: slip stitch

YO: yarn over

( ): work everything inside the parentheses inside the next stitch, e.g. (2 sc) = 2 sc in the next st

[ ]: repeat everything inside the brackets the number of times indicated

INSTRUCTIONS

Small Choux Bun

- With Beige, make magic circle, or ch 3 and sl st to first ch to form ring.

Rnd 1: Ch 1, 6 sc into ring. Don't join rnds. Use a stitch marker. – 6 sts

Rnd 2: (2 sc) 6 times. – 12 sts

Rnd 3: [(2 sc), sc] 6 times. – 18 sts

Rnd 4: [(2 sc), 2 sc] 6 times. – 24 sts

Rnds 5 through 7: Sc evenly around. – 24 sts

Rnd 8: [inv dec, 2 sc] 6 times. – 18 sts

- Start lightly stuffing

Rnd 9: [inv dec, sc] 6 times. – 12 sts

- Stuff some more.

Rnd 10: Inv dec 4 times. Sl st to next st to join. Leave remaining sts unworked. – 8 sts all around

- Break off leaving 6 inches (15 cm) of yarn.
- With a yarn needle, pick up the front loops from remaining 8 sts and pull to close.
- Tie off and weave in ends.
- If your choux buns seem lumpy or lopsided, try rolling them in your hands like a real ball of dough. It can help a lot with distributing the stuffing.

Big Choux Bun

- With Beige, make magic circle, or ch 3 and sl st to first ch to form ring.

Rnds 1 through 4: Repeat Rnds 1 through 4 of Small Choux Bun.

Rnd 5: [(2 sc), 3 sc] 6 times. – 30 sts

Rnd 6: [(2 sc), 9 sc] 3 times. – 33 sts

Rnds 7 through 10: Sc evenly around. – 33 sts

Rnd 8: [inv dec, 9 sc] 3 times. – 30 sts

Rnd 9: [inv dec, 3 sc] 6 times. – 24 sts

Rnd 10: [inv dec, 2 sc] 6 times. – 18 sts

- Start lightly stuffing.

Rnd 11: [inv dec, sc] 6 times. – 12 sts

- Stuff some more.

Rnd 12: Inv dec 4 times. Sl st to next st to join. Leave remaining sts unworked. – 8 sts all around

- Break off leaving 6 inches (15 cm) of yarn.
- With a yarn needle, pick up the front loops from remaining 8 sts and pull to close.
- Tie off and weave in end.

Small Icing

- With Light Blue, make magic circle, or ch 3 and sl st to first ch to form ring.

Rnds 1 through 6: Repeat Rnds 1 through 6 of Small Choux Bun. Sl st to next st to join. – 24 sts

- Break off leaving 18 inches (46 cm) of yarn for sewing later. Weave in other end.
- The Small Icing should fit right over the Small Choux Bun like a hat. If it feels too snug, try crocheting the Small Icing with a slightly looser tension or go up one hook size.

Big Icing

- With Light Blue, make magic circle, or ch 3 and sl st to first ch to form ring.

Rnds 1 through 10: Repeat Rnds 1 through 10 of Big Choux Bun. Sl st to next st to join. – 33 sts

- Break off leaving 18 inches (46 cm) of yarn for sewing later. Weave in other end.

Buttercream Collar

- With Natural, ch 36. This should be enough chains to wrap around the widest circumference of the Small Choux Bun about one and a third times.

Row 1: Sk first ch from hook, (2 sc) in each remaining ch. The piece should start forming a curl. After the final sc, sl st into the same ch as the final sc. – 70 sts

- Break off leaving about 6 inches (15 cm) of yarn tail.
- Make sure that the coils look good (you'll probably have to twist and adjust) and sew the ends of the coils together to form a curly ring. Weave in both yarn ends. (A)

Buttercream Dollop

- With Natural, ch 7. This is just a teeny version of the Buttercream Collar.

Row 1: Sk first ch from hook, (2 sc) in each remaining ch. After the final sc, sl st into the same ch as the final sc. – 12 sts

- Break off leaving about 6 inches (15 cm) of yarn tail.
- You don't have to form a ring with this curl. You can shape this dollop however you like and secure the shape with some stitches. Tie a knot to secure. (B)
- You can use the remainder of the long yarn tail to sew the Dollop on later, or you can weave in both ends if you plan to glue.

Assembly

1 Sew the Buttercream Dollop to the top of Small Icing. (C) It's easier to attach this now while you have access to the underside of the icing. If you plan to glue the dollop, you can do that after Step 5.

2 Center Small Icing on top of Small Choux Bun, making sure Small Icing is smooth and fitting snuggly. Use a gentle running stitch to sew the edge of the icing around the bun. Don't pull stitches too tightly or you might pinch the shape of the bun and icing. Tie a knot and bury the yarn tail inside the bun. (D)

3 Repeat Step 2 with Big Icing and Big Choux Bun.

4 Attach Small Choux Bun to the top of Big Choux Bun. You can use hot glue here if you wish, as this join will be mostly covered by the Buttercream Collar. Or you can sew the buns together with yarn. My preferred method is to string them together like giant beads. Get a long piece of Beige yarn. String it from the bottom center (or 0.25 inch / 6 mm off center) of Big Choux Bun, all the way through the top center of it, then travel your needle through the bottom center of Small Choux Bun, taking a "bite" of it approximately 0.5 inch (1.5 cm) wide. (Don't go through the top of Small Choux Bun.) Then go back down the top center (or 0.25 inch / 6 mm off center) of Big Choux Bun, and through the bottom center of Big Choux Bun just about 0.5 inch (1.5 cm) away from where your original yarn tail is. (E) Playing with the tension of the yarn before tying a knot, so that you know the stack is secure, but also so that the buns don't appear too squished. I do like a slight squishing at the bottom because it helps stabilize the religieuse. You might also need to try stringing the buns a few times to get everything as centered as you like. When you're ready, tie a square knot at the bottom and hide the yarn ends in the bun.

5 Slip the Buttercream Collar over the top of Small Choux Bun, so that it settles in the join between the buns. Arrange and even out the coils. You don't have to sew or glue this down.

6 If you want to add some sparkle, gently brush on some super fine or edible glitter onto the Icing areas. You can also add small faux pearls or small metallic balls with Loctite Super Glue Ultra Gel or Gem-Tac.

7 Set on a small plate and enjoy your creation.

Twinkie Chan is a San Francisco-based crochet designer known for her colorful, food-themed accessories like cupcake scarves, hamburger mitts, and slushee cup purses. She has published two crochet books, and her work has been featured in craft and lifestyle magazines all over the world since 2006. Some of the companies that Twinkie has collaborated with include Lion Brand yarn, Lily Sugar 'n Cream yarn, Sesame Workshop, Pocky, McDonald's, and Sanrio. She has also worked with the Craft Yarn Council for many years, donating patterns and video tutorials to their annual #stitchawaystress campaign as well their #stitchedwithsweets campaign with the Hallmark Channel in 2023. You can currently see her work in person in Dallas, TX where her bakery-themed crochet installation Sucre Fleuf! has been on view since 2020 at the immersive art museum Sweet Tooth Hotel. When she's not creating deliciously whimsical crocheted creations, Twinkie is an artist coach, instructor, and content producer at Creativebug.com. You can see more of her work on Instagram at @twinkiechan and on etsy.com/shop/twinkiechan and youtube.com/twinkiechantv.

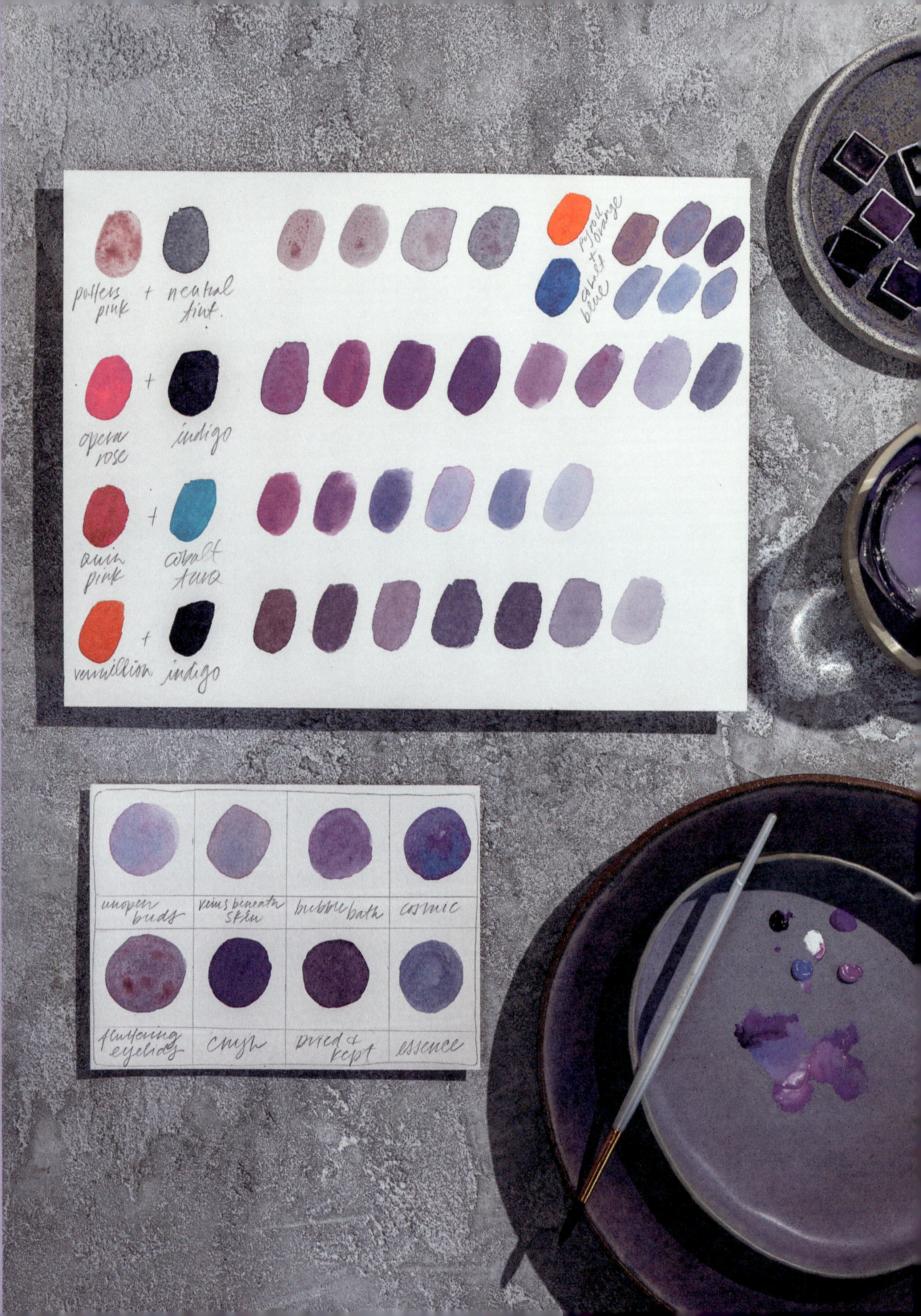
potters pink + neutral tint.
pyrrol orange + cobalt blue
opera rose + indigo
quin pink + cobalt turq
vermillion + indigo
unopen buds
veins beneath skin
bubble bath
cosmic
fluttering eyelids
crush
dried & kept
essence

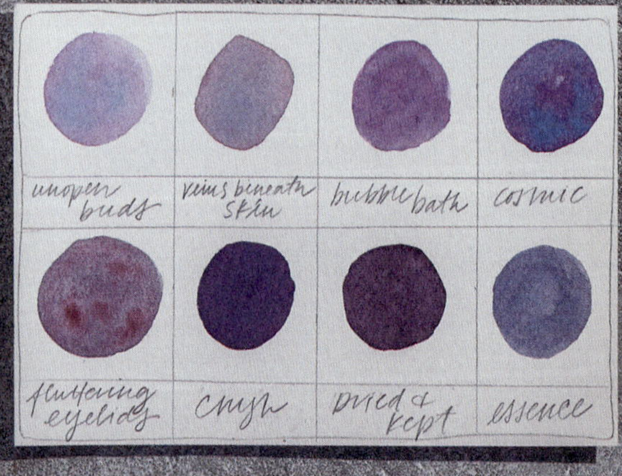

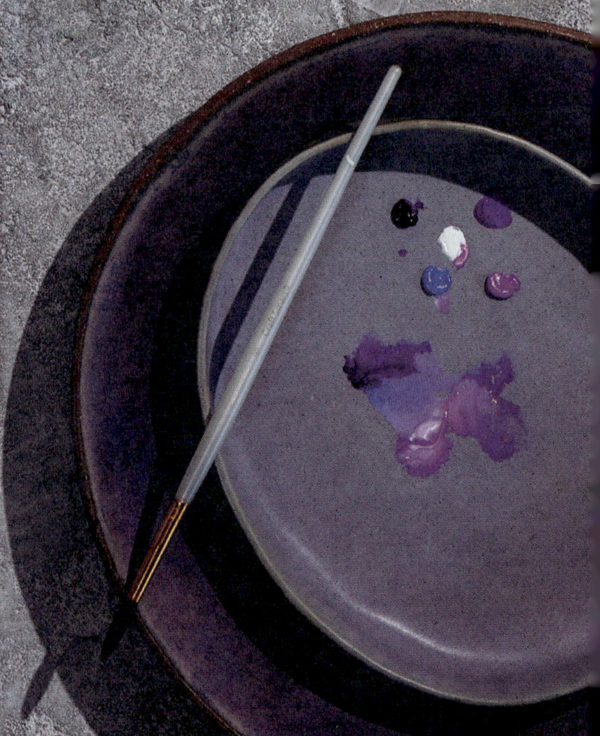

LAVENDER: Finding Lavender Paint Project

CREATED BY

Courtney Cerruti

"Art and craft have always been one fluid thing for me; they go hand-in-hand in my daily life, my art practice, and my professional work. When I was in my twenties, I would go to museums and see monumental works like the twisting metal walls of Richard Serra or the performance-based work of Marina Abramović and think, 'if this is art *then I'm not sure I'm an artist.' I couldn't conceive how I fit into the art world as someone who painted pictures, made small things with my hands, or played with paper and books as an artform. As I continued forging a path as an artist (as I saw it), I began to realize how my artistic vision and handwork could work and live together, how they served one another.*

Now, in my forties, I still make many things and one of my main forms of expression is through watercolor. It's a medium that wouldn't have been taken seriously by museums and galleries even a hundred years ago. It was a sketching medium; a way of rendering ideas; a process, not a final painting medium worthy of display and prestige. Today I can go into a museum and see sketchbooks, watercolor paintings, and even palettes on display. We're seeing the tide turn on what is considered as and has value as ART. The lines between art and craft are blurring. I don't think museums are necessarily leading the change. Rather, I think they are a reflection of how artists approach art making today, how they combine varying practices and interests into art forms that reflect their lives and experiences."

Watercolor painting is easily one of the oldest artforms we know of. Technically, any pigment in a water-based binder can be labeled watercolor paint. This means we can view prehistoric cave paintings, Egyptian tomb and temple paintings, and Chinese and Japanese brush paintings on silks and paper, as all being watercolors. Historically, old master artists often used watercolors to create sketches for larger works, or as a means to quickly get an idea down. Watercolors dry faster than oil paints. They are easily portable, hence their use *en plein air* (painting outdoors in a landscape). They are painted on paper, much easier to procure and carry around than canvas.

In the eighteenth century in England, watercolor became associated with aristocracy and education. Thus watercolor became the tool of documenters—field studies for all the sciences were done in watercolor, as well as illustrations of landmarks, landscapes, and surroundings. Watercolor also became the medium of art hobbyists—think ladies painting roses. But it was also still used by many prominent artists to develop their styles, for faster or smaller versions of their work, or in their drawings.

In twentieth century art, when the very large-scale works of Abstract Expressionism came into favor, watercolor appeared to be further relegated to the back burner. In the twenty-first century, however, watercolor has become a darling of many. Its properties allow both for an incredible precise, slow-layered realism or for a process-oriented, free flowing abstraction. While it's portability, ease of clean-up, and amazing array of colors and formulas invite anyone to dabble with it.

MATERIALS

- Watercolor paper or sketchbook (see resources, below)
- Watercolor brush size 8 or 10 (see resources, below)
- Plate or palette for mixing
- Water
- Paper towel
- Pencil
- Favorite pan or tube watercolors to swatch along with including red, orange, blue, indigo, pink, or others (see resources, below for my exact colors)

RESOURCES

- Fluid hot press watercolor pad, 9-by-12 inches (23-by-30.5 cm)
- I'm using Simply Simmons brush, size 10
- My exact colors: Potter's Pink, Opera Rose, Indigo, Cobalt Turquoise, Neutral Tint, Quinacrodone (Quin) Pink, Organic Vermillion, Pyrrol Orange, Cobalt Blue

A note about watercolor: I have three favorite brands of watercolor that comprise most of my palettes: Schmincke, Daniel Smith, and Winsor & Newton professional. These are all high-quality paints with high pigment load and are sold in tubes and half pans. I also love picking up a color here or there made by other small-batch producers like Case for Making (their neons are the best), Kremer, A Gallo, and others. A basic set of watercolors will work for most painting and swatch play. If you are just starting out, I recommend the W&N Cotman pocket palette which is less than $30 for twelve colors and will get you painting and playing without a large monetary investment. Once you are comfortable with watercolor and curious to explore other brands and colors, you can build your collection from there.

INSTRUCTIONS

Mixing and swatching paint is one of my favorite ways to play with watercolor. It scratches the itch to paint even when I don't have a subject in mind. It allows me to play with color, saturation, and combinations in unexpected ways that always delight and surprise me.

In 2017 I made a watercolor sketchbook into a daily swatching diary, where I mixed and painted a color and added a line of text to mark the passing of each day. This practice was highly satisfying, and it was the inspiration for my book, *One Color a Day: A Daily Practice and Visual Diary.*

In that vein I want to share the joy of "finding colors" by mixing unexpected combinations to discover the color lavender. Of course, we could just mix red and blue together and add a little water, but where's the fun in that?

1 I begin with Potter's Pink, an earthy and subtle pink tone that can range in color from brand to brand and mix it with one of my favorites, Neutral Tint, a grey color that can often lean to the cooler side.

2 With a wet brush, dip into your Potter's Pink, adding water and mixing the paint as needed to fill your brush. Then "paint" this color onto your palette, making a large pool of color. Next, paint a swatch onto your paper and label the color. Your swatch can be a messy blob, a circle, a brush stroke, or whatever shape you like. Make sure the swatch represents the color well and isn't too light (too much water) or too dark and sticky (not enough water). Rinse your brush and do the same with Neutral Tint, making your pool of color next to Potters Pink and making a swatch on your paper. Rinse your brush again. (A)

3 With a clean brush, dip into the Neutral Tint just a little and add it to your PP, mix slightly to form a new color, and paint a swatch of this onto your paper. You can label these mixes if you choose or not. Continue adding a little more Neutral Tint and a smidge of water as needed to make new color, swatching them as you go until you find a color you would call "lavender." (B)

A

B
potters pink + neutral tint

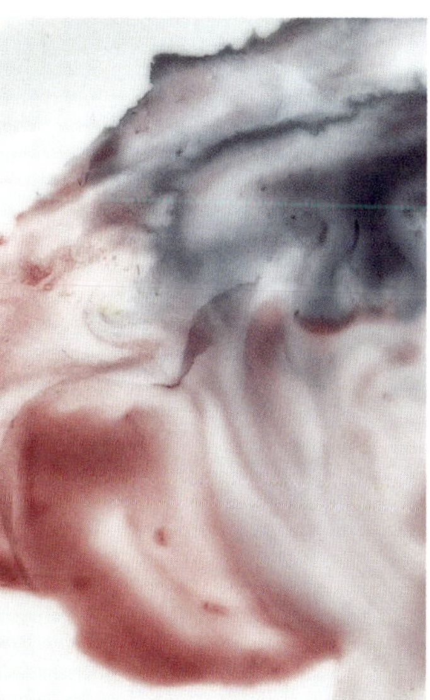

C

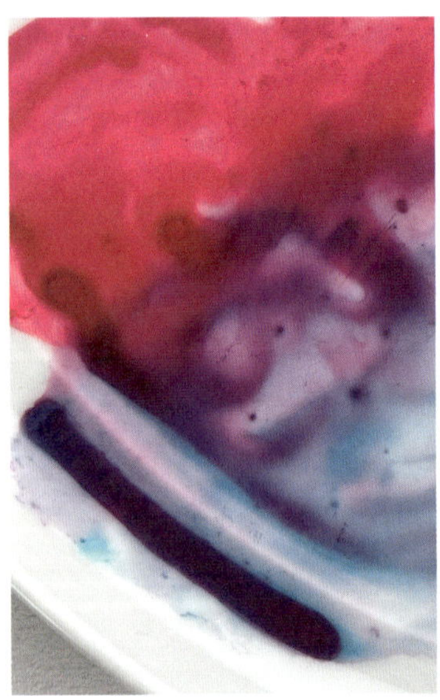

D

4 With a clean brush, start the process again, this time using two of my all-time favorite colors, Opera Rose (as hot pink as you can go without using a fluorescent paint) and Indigo. (C)

5 Repeat the above steps, playing with saturation of paint, water, and mixing. Swatch each new color you mix as you go. (D)

6 The other unexpected color pairings I tried and you can as well are: (E)

- Quinacridone Pink + Cobalt Turquoise
- Organic Vermillion + Indigo
- Pyrrol Orange + Cobalt Blue

7 If you'd like to make a swatch card of all the "lavenders" you've found and name them with your own special connotations or color names, you can do this on a separate piece of watercolor paper or in your sketchbook. I eyeballed a grid onto paper that included eight spots for swatches and eight small boxes for text below each color. (F)

I found . . .

- Unopen buds
- Veins beneath skin
- Bubble bath
- Cosmic
- Fluttering eyelids
- Crush
- Dried & kept
- Essence

Courtney Cerruti is an artist, author, collaborator, and educator. Courtney has authored five books including *Make Art Where You Are* and *One Color a Day*. She teaches workshops all over the country and online at Creativebug.com where she is Editor-In-Chief. Her work has been featured on Oh Happy Day, Design Sponge, the *San Francisco Chronicle*, Instagram, *Uppercase* Magazine, The Jealous Curator, and BuzzFeed among others. She makes something every day and can be found on Instagram as @ccerruti and at courtneycerruti.com.

CREATED BY

e bond

PURPLE: Accordion Book

"My exploration of purple is a mono-printed meandering one-sheet accordion. Some call these forms 'flutter books' or 'single-sheet folded books.' Whatever you call it, I like this form because you start with a large piece of paper and then fold it down into a book form. It's fun to see what happens to the content on the original page by folding and compressing its form. My single sheet started its life as an 18-by-24-inch (46 by 61 cm) mixed-media drawing paper, on which I made a series of layered mono prints on top of one another. And then, of course, the final folded book ended up much smaller. Using forms like this allows me first to create freely on the page, seeing it very clearly one way; and then let go and watch it abstract itself as I cut and fold the paper down into another different form entirely.

Of course, you don't have to be as freewheeling with this form as I chose to be. You could plan out where everything goes ahead of time so you know what will happen when it's folded. I've certainly used that method before as well. But I thought for something like exploring color, why not just allow the book to do what it's going to do with the art I created? Why not see where that takes me with purple?"

Before there were books, there were scrolls. Scrolls predate books by about two millennia, showing up in ancient Egypt circa 2400 B.C.E. Books as we know them today—paper bound between two covers—began to make their appearance in the Greek and Roman empires around 500 B.C.E. Before the advent of the printing press in the middle ages, hand-lettered and illustrated books became a way to preserve and share important knowledge, with monks lettering religious texts one copy at a time.

Truth be told, there are *so many ways* to make and bind a book. Google book binding and you can easily become overwhelmed—stapling vs. sewn, perfect vs. spiral binding, leather vs. paper bound. The fact of the matter is though, that there are some very simple ways to make a book. And making your own book can offer a lot of freedom. You can publish a single copy of a single thought. Or produce a zine to share far and wide.

You can create blank books to be your sketchbooks, and then fill them with diary entries or collages. You can create books made from artworks themselves—folding and cutting single sheets of pre-printed, pre-stamped, pre-painted paper to make up your book's pages. Books are often revered and still hold prominence in our society from manuals to philosophy. Even in digital form, books are still how we learn. The possibilities are so vast and exciting when you're able to create a book from scratch, especially when you control the contents.

MATERIALS

- 1 large piece of sturdy yet flexible paper (see resources, below)
- Bone folder
- Ruler
- Utility/precision knife or scissors
- Art supplies to decorate your paper, I used acrylic paints and a gel plate to make monoprints all over my paper on both sides.
- Paint scraper, I used to make abstract marks (optional)
- Letter stencils (optional)

If you are making covers you will also need:

- 2 pieces of book board
- PVA (glue)
- Brush or roller and tray (for gluing)
- Scrap paper for gluing
- 2 other pieces of decorated paper to cover your boards

RESOURCES

- I like 98-pound Canson mixed media paper. I used an 18–by-24-inch (46 by 61 cm) piece, but you can go larger or smaller if you like.

INSTRUCTIONS

1 Decorate your large sheet of paper however you want. You can choose to focus on one side only or decorate both sides as in my example. Feel free to experiment with any materials/themes/imagery/colors you like. (A, B, C, D) Whatever you choose to do, just make sure your paper is thoroughly dry before beginning to fold your paper into the book form.

2 Fold your paper in half, then unfold. (E) Take one side edge of the paper (right or left) and fold that into the center. Next, take the opposite edge of the paper and fold that side into the center as well. (F, G) You should see four equal sections. Unfold your paper.

3 Rotate your paper 90 degrees and repeat the same fold pattern until you have four equal sections this way as well. (H, I, J, K) By the end of this step you should have sixteen equal folded sections on your paper. (L)

A

B

C

D

E

F

G

H

I

J

K

L

4 Cut your paper. Make sure you orient your paper vertically in front of you. You are going to make three cuts, following the diagram below.

5 Lay your ruler along Fold Line A (the top fold), but you are only going to cut to the third fold. (M) Never cut all the way through the paper on any of your cuts. Your paper should remain in one piece even after the three cuts have been made. Make sure your cut stops where you see the black circle.

6 After cutting Fold Line A, repeat for Fold Line B (middle fold) and Fold Line C (fold closest to you). (N, O) You should have three cuts in your paper when you are done this step. (P)

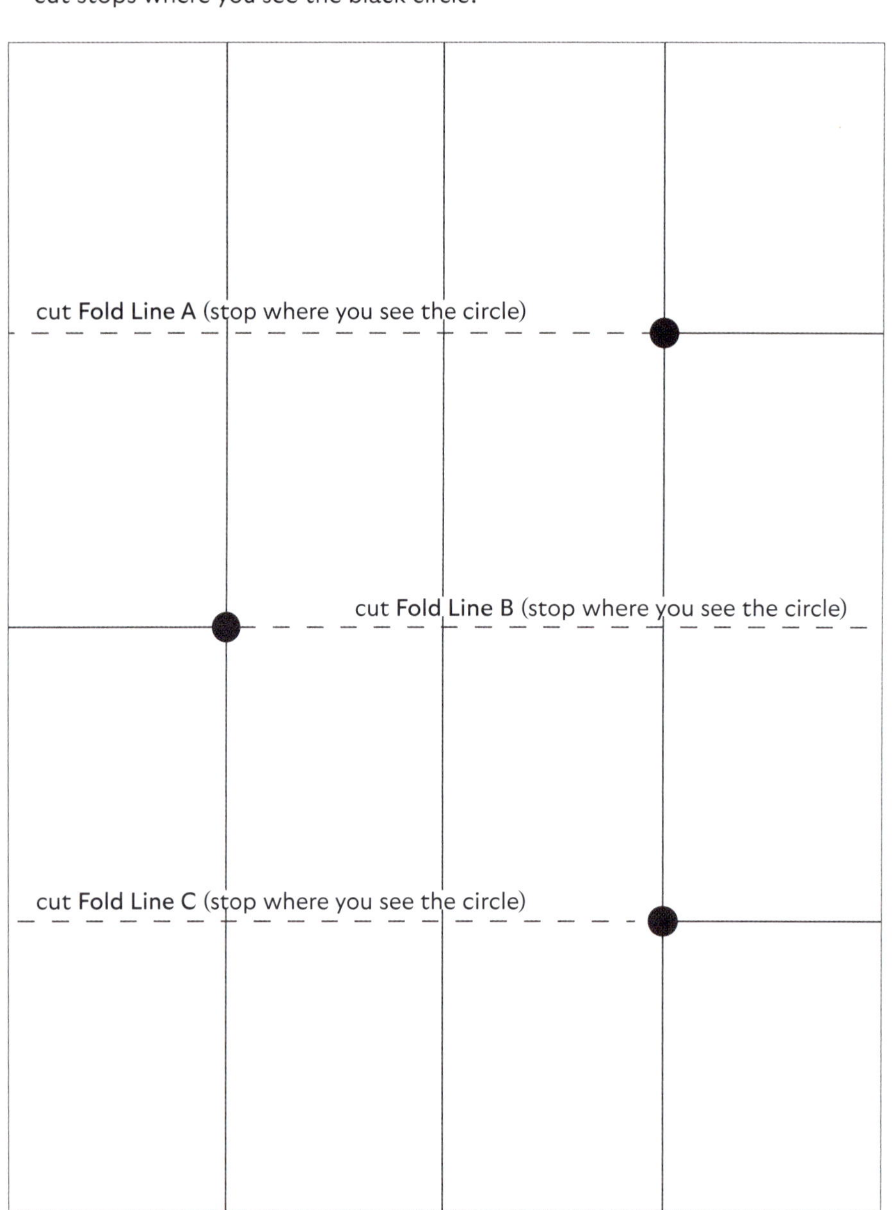

M
Artist's Loft

N

O
Artist's Loft

P

Q
R
S
T
U
V
W
X
Y

7 Start from the left side of your large paper and start accordion folding the paper back and forth. (Q, R, S) When you get to an end of a row, bend the pages down and behind the paper (T), and then continue folding back and forth in this same motion. (U, V, W, X, Y, Z, AA, BB, CC, DD) You now have a finished book without covers. (EE)

Z

AA

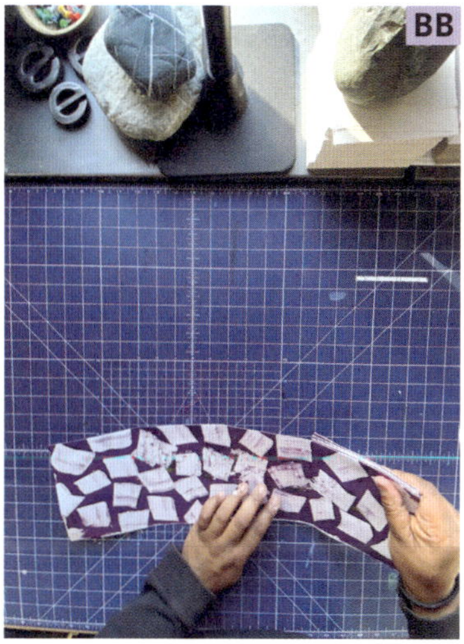

BB

CC

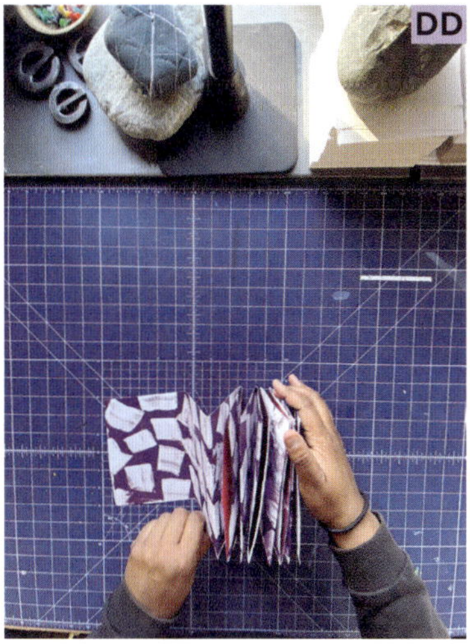

DD

EE

8 At this point you'll notice a few areas in the folded book that have two pieces of paper that come together as sort of flaps. You can decide to glue these down to one another or leave them as is. In my example, I have glued mine down. This offers a bit of stability and makes more of a traditional book. (FF, GG, HH)

These flaps can be glued together

Adding Covers to the Book (optional):

To figure out the size of boards you will need as covers, measure your finished book. Once you have those measurements, add 0.25 inch (6 mm) to the height and the width of your book's measurements. (For example, if your accordion book is 4-by-6 inches / 10 by 15 cm, your boards will need to be 4.25-by-6.25 inches / 11 by 16 cm.)

1 Using your ruler and utility/precision knife, carefully cut two boards the size you have determined from Step 1.

2 Next, cut two pieces of decorated paper 0.75 inch (2 cm) larger than the board you are covering on each side. A total of 1.5 inches (4 cm) should be added to the height and width of the board measurement. (For example, if your board is 4.25-by-6.25 inches / 11 by 16 cm, your paper should be 5.75-by-7.75 inches / 14.5 by 19.5 cm).

3 Using a brush or roller, put a small amount of glue on the board evenly. If using a brush, start in the center of the board with the glue brushing outward towards the edges of the board.

4 Take the board with glue on it and center it in the middle of the decorated paper (decorated paper should be face down on your table). (II, step a) Smooth down the paper using the bone folder, going from the middle out to the edge to remove any bubbles.

5 Clip the paper diagonally approximately ⅛ inch (3 mm) away from the board on each corner. (II, step b)

6 Put glue on the top and bottom tabs making sure it is completely covered. Use a minimal amount of glue to minimize excess squeezing out. (II, step c) Use the bone folder to burnish, glue down each tab, one by one.

7 Glue the two opposite sides—using the bone folder or your fingernail, pinch corners in before folding the tabs down with the bone folder. (II, step d)

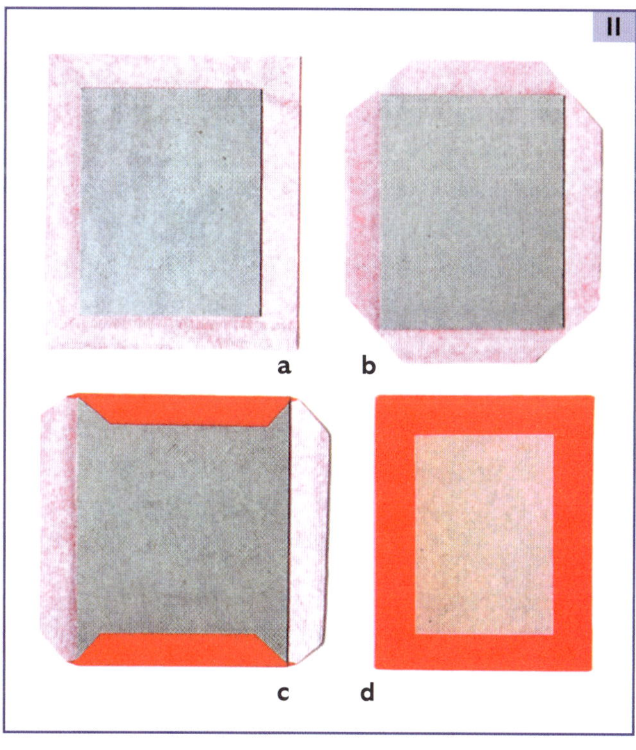

8 Repeat steps 4 through 8 on your second board until you have two covers for your book.(JJ)

9 Once both covers are covered, glue your book onto the covers. Use scrap paper in between the page you are gluing and the rest of the book to ensure excess glue doesn't spread onto your book. Glue up the book page, *not the cover*. Then center that whole book onto the first cover. Once it is centered, use your bone folder to burnish it down. Glue the back cover the same way.

JJ

e bond works in design spaces by day, makes handmade books by night, hangs out with trees on weekends, and writes something close to poems in the spaces between. Under the studio name roughdrAftbooks, created in 2003, she makes one-of-a-kind art books, printed pieces, and abstract drawings that merge and blur the boundaries of art, craft, surface design, and poetry. e holds a BFA in graphic design and art history from Moore College of Art & Design and an MFA in Creative Writing and Book Arts from Mills College. For over 25 years, e has worked as a print and web designer while also serving as professor of Graphic Design and Book Art in various college and university art departments. Her work is held in library collections across the United States and has been published in numerous books (about books). Most recently, e's work has moved into the wonderful world of surface design where she has designed many colorful, abstract fabric collections in collaboration with Free Spirit Fabrics. You can see her work at ebondwork.com and on Instagram at @eisroughdraft.

BLACK: Air Dry Clay Dishes

CREATED BY

Kim Nguyen

"Once I knew I was using the color black, I knew I also wanted to incorporate gold as an accent color. I really love the contrast that black creates. I wanted to make a project that was quick and accessible, but easily customizable with paint, so I chose trinket dishes. When I think of black, I immediately think of nighttime. Some of my favorite nighttime creatures are moths, and I love the variation in them and how beautiful they are. Making multiple dishes each featuring a different type of moth seemed fitting."

The history of ceramics is vast—with pottery dating back to 18,000 BCE and a ceramic statuette dating to 28,000 BCE. Since almost the dawn of humanity, we have found a way to fire dirt clay into objects. But making ceramics at home is a bit more challenging. There are kilns, different kinds of clay bodies and glazes to contend with. There is a serious investment involved in setting up a home ceramics studio, or finding a pottery class or space to work in. Modern formulations of air dry and paper clay are super easy to use, dry fairly quickly, and allow people to make ceramic-like items without the need for fancy accoutrements.

Air dry clay formulations usually contain a clay body with additional additives like corn starch, cellulose, and wood or cotton fibers. It dries evenly, usually without cracking, and hardens to a similar consistency as bisque fired clay (this is clay before it's been glazed). While it isn't naturally waterproof or usable as dishware to eat off of, it can be drawn or painted on and sealed, as seen here. This preserves your piece and makes it more substantial. A larger, sealed air dry bowl could certainly hold fruit on a countertop.

As with ceramics, there are many forms to make with air dry clay—wall hangings, beads, large sculptures, decorative dishware. It's such a versatile medium that we asked two artists to create a "functional" and a "decorative" project for this book. This is the functional one, for the decorative one see page 217.

MATERIALS

- Air-dry clay
- Rolling pin
- Water
- Small craft knife
- Acrylic paint
- Paintbrushes
- Gloss glaze (see resources, below)
- Two wooden craft sticks/silicone sculpting tool (optional but helpful)

RESOURCES

- Deco Art Triple Thick Gloss Glaze - https://shop.decoart.com/triple-thick-gloss-glaze/

INSTRUCTIONS

1 Prepare the clay by rolling it out to about a 0.25 inch (6 mm) thick. I use two wooden sticks to help ensure an even thickness throughout, but you can eyeball. (A, B)

2 Using an overturned bowl or paper template, cut out a circle from the clay. If you're making a walled dish, also cut out a long rectangle of clay, approximately as long as the circumference of your circle. (C, D)

3 Dampen your fingers with a bit of water and smooth out the edges of your dishes. (E)

A

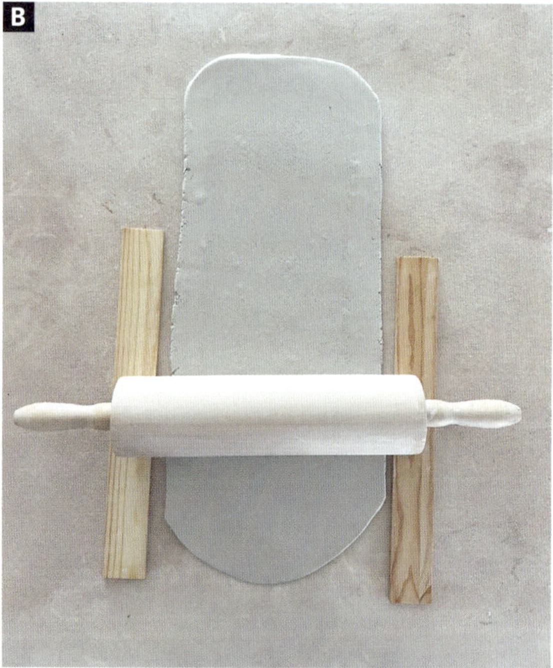
B

C

D

E

4 For the walled dish, score and slip* around your circle base, as well as the bottom of the long rectangle. (F, G) Join the pieces together by holding firmly together. (H, I) Then smooth out the edges and joints, either with your fingers or a silicone sculpting tool as needed. (J, K) If your rectangle isn't long enough to cover the entire circumference, just add an additional piece as needed. Any areas where clay will be joined together should be scored and slipped before joining.

5 For the smaller dishes, use your index fingers and thumbs to create a slight upturned lip by pinching and rotating around the entire dish. (L, M)

*Score and slip: Use a craft knife to score little cuts into the clay where you will be joining pieces together. The slip can be made by mixing pieces of clay with water to create a gloopy consistency. Brush a little slip on all scored areas.

H

I

J

K

L

M

6 Leave to dry overnight/few days. You will know when the clay is dry when it is even and matte with no variation in color (usually this means it's bright white and no longer looks a little gray or wet) and completely dry to the touch. Once the clay is completely dry, paint each dish with acrylic paint. You can paint a single color, or create a design, a pattern, or focus on a theme like insects. (N, O, P)

7 After paint has dried fully, apply a thick coat of gloss glaze to seal and protect the paint. (Q)

Kim Nguyen is a hobby ceramicist from San Diego, California. When she's not busy owning and running a math and reading program and working with amazing kids, she can be found in her home studio. While she dabbles in many arts and crafts, from sewing to painting and printmaking, nothing has made as big an impression as working with clay. Introduced to ceramics in high school, she's been jumping on and off the wheel ever since. Incorporating her love of drawing, stenciling, and screen printing, Kim creates ceramic work that often reflects her Vietnamese culture. Most of her work's inspiration comes from the strong women in her life—her mother, sister, aunties, and cousins. You can find her work on Instagram @blackslipbabes.

I CAN'T TAKE THE PAIN AWAY...

BUT I CAN SIT WITH YOU IN IT.

Carissa Potter '24

GRAY: Drawing Through Anxiety

CREATED BY

Carissa Potter

"When I was young, I was labeled 'sensitive.' Sensitive can mean lots of things. To me, it somehow implied that I was both difficult and artistic. How do the stories we are told about ourselves shape us as children? I don't really know. But I am a person who uses art to process emotions. We are a species that makes things and feels things. Because of my genetics or upbringing—or my observations of the world right now—I have a lot of anxiety. It's probably the norm at the moment. Anxiety is definitely having a moment. I was first diagnosed with an anxiety disorder when I was ten. I worried that I was obsessing over things and annoying people. People in my life would feel the need to fix me. Or they would tell me that I should just feel better. These things did not help. I just wanted someone to listen—I needed to process what was going on in my head, when it was going on. But often I was alone. And so I started drawing the situations to explore them.

The really great thing about art is that you don't have to have any conclusions. You can just make things and feel things and let that be that. Now, to be sure, there are people who are going to say that they have rules: You must have a concept first. Or it must be beautiful. Or it is only worth something if someone else is willing to pay for it. All of this is true if you believe it to be true. But I don't. Making is an act of hope. An act of faith that something better is out there, that we can evolve and grow and endure. It is also a tool to understand and communicate. I want to feel things as deeply and as truthfully as possible. Why not combine our feelings and our making and see how it makes us feel? See how it allows us to connect?"

Teaching drawing is something I love to do. When I first started creating syllabi for drawing classes, almost twenty years ago, I would include the following, and it still rings true to me:

Drawing has been the most basic of all art skills from prehistoric times to the present. It is essential to all art and design disciplines: painting, sculpture, printmaking, fine crafts, architecture, interior design, industrial design, fashion design, and even for the performing arts such as theater and dance.

Drawing is the most democratic of all art forms. It is a common denominator for people worldwide. Drawings are valued for their accessibility, their intimacy, and their use in working through ideas. This last is called visual thinking, and alongside much practice at making and looking at drawings comes a more evolved stage of visual literacy.

The process of drawing develops a heightened awareness of the visual world. This awareness is both subjective (knowing how you feel about things) and objective (understanding how things actually operate). Drawing provides a new format for stating what you already know about the world and a new system for learning about and understanding what you don't. Drawing teaches you to observe, distinguish, and relate.

Even if you can't find the time to do anything else Artistic with a capital A, you can always draw. You can doodle on a scrap of paper, or even draw digitally. Drawing is so immediate, so satisfying. Making marks is a completely human endeavor. If we can't understand one another with language, we can probably draw one another a picture to communicate. Even a "bad" picture can explain a lot. The tools you can draw with are endless: pencils, charcoal, chalk, pens, crayons, oil pastels. Here, Carissa is using sumi ink and a brush, and drawing text. Yes, writing text can be drawing. And if you've never drawn with ink before, it is an extremely pleasurable pursuit and feels different than any other media, especially if you try pen nibs, fountain pens, or Asian calligraphy brushes (and, yes, using a brush can be drawing).

MATERIALS

- Something to write on
- A writing tool
- Sumi ink (watered down to create a gray)
- A container/palette for your gray ink
- Favorite paper in any size (I prefer large sheets, just keep in mind you want paper that can handle water)
- Sumi brush/bamboo calligraphy brush, or your favorite brush
- Clean water
- Rag/paper towels to dab excess ink off brush (optional)

INSTRUCTIONS

1. Rally a word document or a blank journal (or one filled with thoughts), a writing tool (I use a marker and pencil), and also your painting supplies. (A) This is about what feels good and easy for you. Nothing else matters. Grab a warm beverage, or cool one depending on your desired body temperature. Take a few deep long breaths, relaxing your shoulders.
2. Free write down what you are spiraling about (preferably under a full moon). Don't worry how it sounds, what it reads like, no one needs to ever see this. It is about accessing a different part of you, creating distance, a separation between you and your thoughts and emotions. Taking them outside your head and putting them somewhere else.
3. Look through your writing and find a universal truth or think about what you are longing to hear. Highlight that. Or write down the next thing/phrase you think of.
4. Sketch out your text/drawing/whatever on your sheet of paper. (B) Perhaps this is a totally unnecessary step, but I do this before I paint. I do it because I am scared I will screw up. I still believe that intentions matter, and I should have a plan. Sometimes only a little or no plan creates things that are even more interesting and beautiful. If you'd like, add some images that you feel like tell part of the story.

A

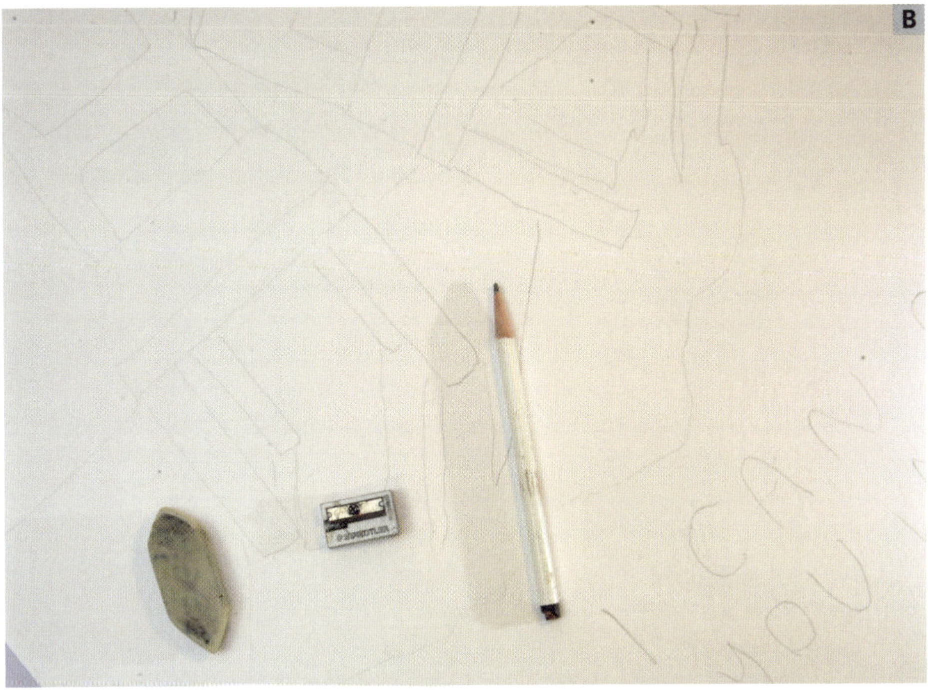
B

5 When you are ready, go ahead and dip that brush in and paint your text, or if you are more comfortable with images, go with that. (C, D, E) If you want to pre-make a gray add drops of sumi ink to plain water until you reach your desired shade. You can also dip your brush into water, into the sumi, and back into water to create variable shades of gray. Blobs and mistakes welcome. Spelling errors mean it was done by a human. You are one. That is so miraculous.

6 Sit with what you have made. Consider sharing it with someone who would feel less alone if they received it. How are you feeling now? Has anything changed inside of you?

7 When you are ready, move on with your day. Or make another anxiety drawing. (F)

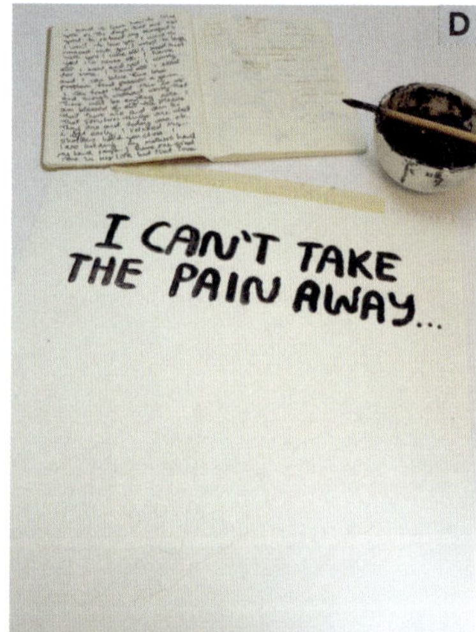

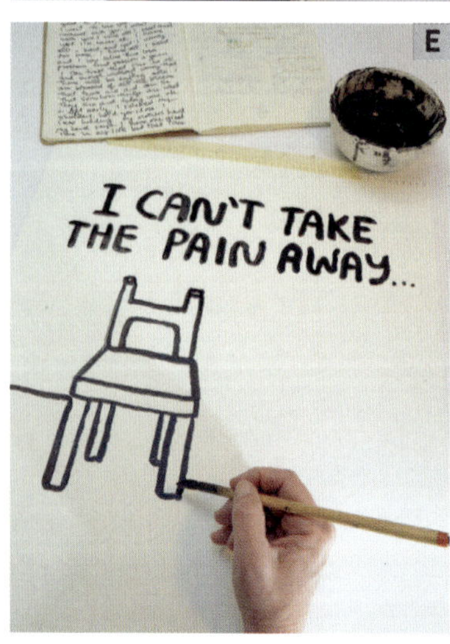

Carissa Potter is a human longing for connection. She writes books, makes art and public commissions, and hosts the series *Bad at Keeping Secrets* (one of Substack's featured newsletters of 2022) where she talks to other humans doing really interesting things. Carissa is the founder of the stationery and gift line People I've Loved. She is the author of four books including *Breath Through It* and *It's Ok to Feel Things Deeply.* And she was one of *Ad Age*'s 24 Most Inspiring People of 2021. She lives in Oakland, California with her partner and daughter and is working on accepting people as they are with love and compassion. You can see her work at peopleiveloved.com and carissapotter.com, on Instagram at @peopleiveloved, and subscribe to her newsletter at peopleiveloved.substack.com.

WHITE: Beaded Wall Hanging

CREATED BY

Jenifer Lake

"My moon, desert, ocean, and natural world ceramics—and this Small Kingdoms series in particular—are all an ongoing exploration of my love for our oceans, the constellations, the solar system, vast landscapes, and our place and relationship within these mysterious wonders of our world. This series is also inspired by the wonderful poem 'Sleeping In the Forest' by Mary Oliver."

For a detailed description of air dry clay, see page 200. Not only can it be used as a medium to be painted and sealed—as we saw in Kim Nguyen's moth bowls project—when left untreated, the natural matte surface of the clay can create a distinct surface that can emulate both traditional ceramics and the natural world. The unaltered color of air dry clay pairs beautifully with wood, shells, leather, etc.

From wall hangings to beads, large sculptures to decorative dishware, the possibilities of this medium are truly endless. Gone are the days when you needed to visit a pottery studio to engage with a clay practice (though, of course, that can be an enjoyable and exciting thing to do, too). This is an easy and versatile medium to use at home.

MATERIALS

- Air-dry clay (any brand will work)
- Variety of tools—ones used in ceramics are great, but chopsticks, small dowels, a butter knife, etc. will work
- Cording to string your beads—leather, rope, ribbon would all work
- Nature bits and bobs for inspiration and adding to the hanging (optional)
- Acrylic paint should you choose to add color (optional)

TIPS

- Your fingers/hands are some of your best tools to shape and mold the clay into interesting forms.
- Any smoothing or buffing of unwanted wrinkles and textures can be accomplished with just a soft touch of your fingers and the *tiniest* bit of water.
- Make more beaded forms and shapes than you think you'll need for your final piece so you have options at the end.

INSTRUCTIONS

1 Work on one shape/bead at a time. Pinch off spheres of air dry clay (approximately 1 to 2 inches / 2.5 to 5 cm wide) to mold into various beads. (A, B) Aim for twenty to thirty shapes.

2 Create some round bead shapes by rolling the clay in the palm of your hands. (C) Then take some round beads and flatten or pinch their ends. (D, E) I often have natural ephemera around while working to inspire the shapes I make.

3 Use a dowel or long pointed tool to pierce a hole through the middle of your bead. (F, G, H) After carefully piercing all the way through, clean-up/smooth the chunky area(s) surrounding the hole with your fingers.

4 If texture is desired, add with a variety of basic clay tools. You can also use things around the house to create textures/scratch. Forks, needles, wooden stylus/sticks, straws, and anything that can be interesting stamping material (fabric, nature, rubber stamps, etc.). (I, J, K, L, M, N, O)

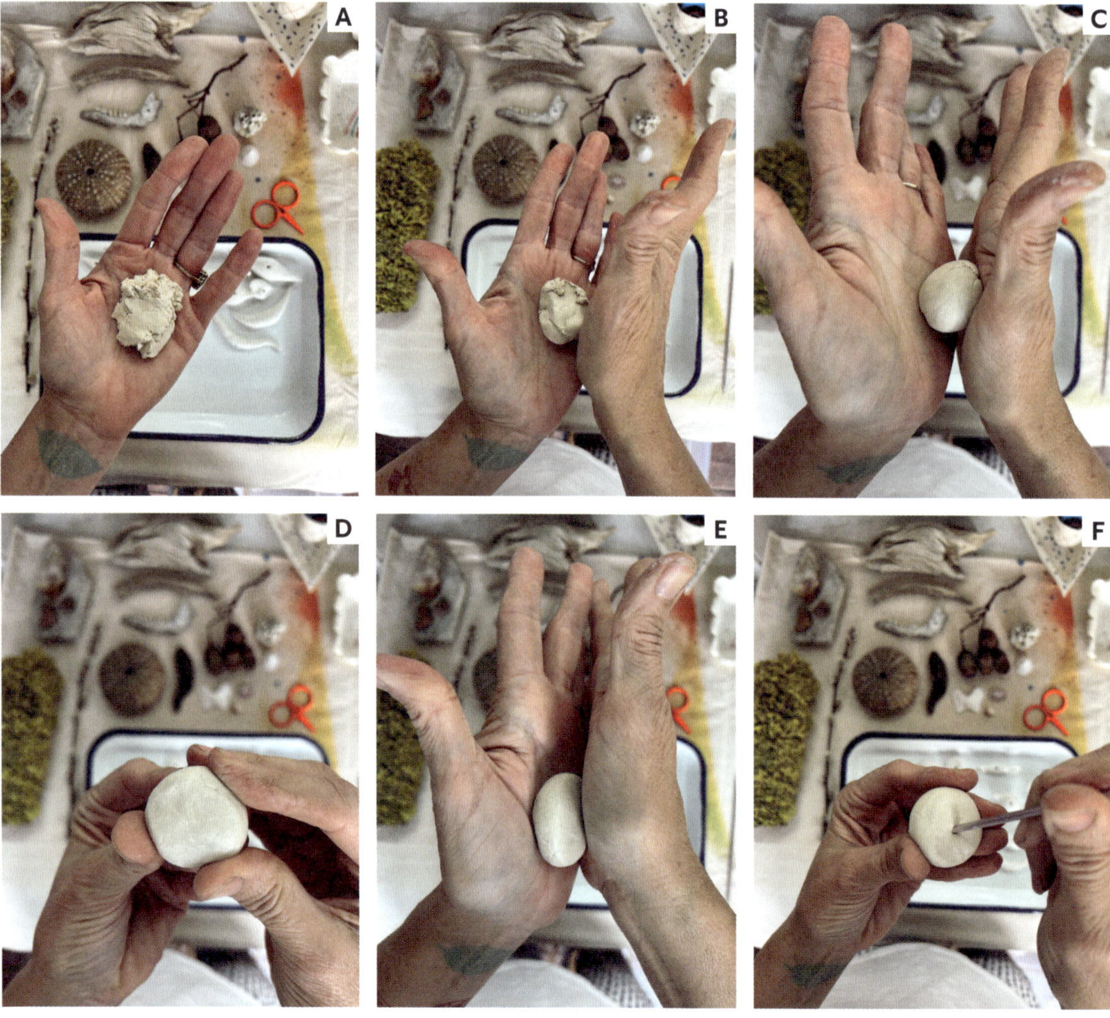

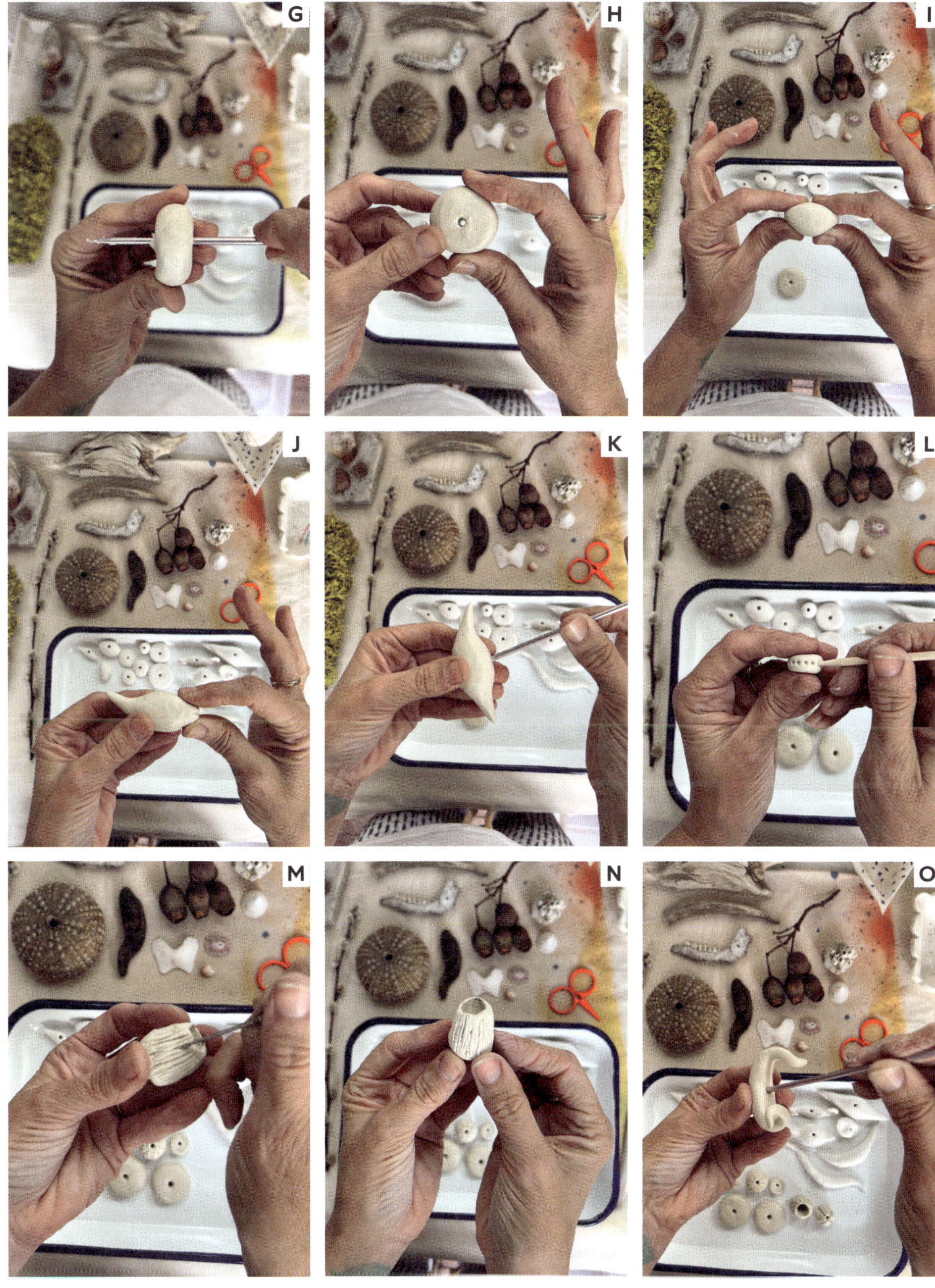
G
H
I
J
K
L
M
N
O

5 After making a variety of beads, let them dry for at least two days. Because of their thickness, it can take up to five days depending on the climate you live in.

6 Once dry, set out all your shapes and play with different arrangements working until you have an aesthetically pleasing collection. (P) You can make long or short ones, plan to hang them vertically or horizontally, or generate chunky necklaces.

7 Secure a knot on the end of your cord of choice—I prefer leather cording for stringing most of my wall hangings. (I double knot depending on the hole size to ensure the bottom bead won't slip off) and begin stringing shapes. (Q)

8 After stringing your desired number of beads and adding any bits of nature (you can drill holes through driftwood or tie on larger bits), I create a loose knotted loop at the top to hang my piece.

Other things to consider

- Air dry clay can be painted in any way for pops of single color or any combination that suits your fancy! (R)
- Cording choices are vast and many; choose what you love aesthetically for your particular piece but keep in mind the strength of the cord and weight of your piece.
- I drilled two pieces of found driftwood to add to the top of my piece but experimented with shells, wood, beach finds, forest finds, or any nature elements. Bright plastic or glass could also be lovely additions.

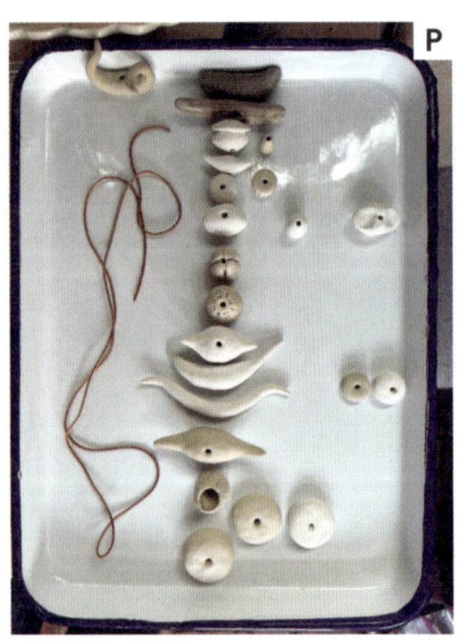
P

Q

R

Jenifer Lake's passion for clay started in middle school when she had access to her first ceramic studio class and fell in deep with the potter's wheel and hand-building. This has continued off and on for just shy of four decades now. She's always learning new ways to expand on her clay adoration and repertoire. A love for well-crafted, yet caringly wabi-sabi handmade pieces inspired by all things in this beautiful, natural world we live in is what Jenifer strives for. She is a creator at heart and has been making and selling art and handmade items since 2003.

Jenifer has been teaching in various settings for over twenty-five years. She's taught at camps, workshops, studios, conferences, and in many classrooms to ages five to over seventy. She is currently a kindergarten through eighth grade visual arts teacher in downtown San Francisco, California. Even though she has a southern heart, and hails from the Southeast originally, she feels lucky to call San Francisco her home and considers California her forever spot. Jenifer has shown her work throughout the United States in many galleries, boutiques, art show exhibitions, and show halls. Her work is in quite a few private collections as well. You can find Jenifer at jeniferlake.com, on Instagram at @jenifer_lake, and on Facebook at jeniferesIake. She can also be reached at jenifer_lake@icloud.com.

IVORY:
Woven Bowl

CREATED BY

Anne Weil

"Use this stunning little bowl to store little essentials or jewelry, or use it to add charm to your table or counter. I love the combination of linen and raffia to form a simple, yet beautiful, coiled bowl. Raffia is a sustainable crop made from the dried, shredded leaves of Raffia Palm trees native to Madagascar. Using raffia as the core of the basket creates a light-weight and yet incredibly sturdy structure. Adding a simple handle provides a cohesive additional element to complement the overall form and function of the bowl. What I love about this technique is its versatility! Once you know the basics, play with form and shape to create vessels of different sizes and types. Make it huge or tiny, add a cover, or make the shape less uniform—or any number of other modifications you can dream up. For instance, changing the width of your bundle creates a different texture. Add color shapes to your basket design or color block it by simply wrapping with a new color wherever you desire."

Basically, for as long as there have been humans there has been weaving. In the Paleolithic era, baskets were woven out of grass, stems, and parts of trees. People wove roofs for shelter and fencing, clothing for warmth and decoration, rugs to sit on, and more. The simplest forms of weaving can be done without any tools—just a weaver's hands and the right materials. But, inevitably, as tools like needles and looms were invented, weaving became more complex.

Almost every culture around the globe has a traditional weaving pattern or technique that has been passed down for millennia. And, as with many other crafts, people's willingness to accept weaving as a fine art has waxed and waned over the years. There is currently a resurgence of popular interest in weaving with kits of materials and workshops readily available for anyone to try.

Weaving easily moves from large to small scale. It is also quite simple to make looms and shuttles from cardboard, scraps of wood, etc. And unless you are using the largest, most complex looms—multi-warp, foot-peddled, the size of a large piece of furniture—most basic weaving techniques are easy enough to be completed by a young child. This low entry threshold allows almost anyone to give it a try. Home weavers can experiment with natural materials and fibers. Or they can go all-out mixed-media and incorporate wire, strips of cloth, flashy yarns, beads, or any other material that can be run over and under a warp. Whether your weaving is functional or decorative is entirely up to you.

MATERIALS

- Two 2-ounce (50 g) bundles of raffia (see resources, below)
- One 200-yard spool tow linen (see resources, below)
- Sharp thread clippers/scissors
- Sharp 7 cm darning needle (see resources, below)

Final measurements:

6.25 inches (16 cm) long by 5.5 inches (14 cm) wide by 1.5 inches (4 cm) tall

RESOURCES

- Flax & Twine Natural Raffia: https://flaxandtwine.com/products/natural-raffia-fiber
- Flax & Twine Tow Linen: https://flaxandtwine.com/products/tow-linen-1-5-1
- 7 cm Darning Needle: https://flaxandtwine.com/products/flax-twine-sharp-darning-needle

INSTRUCTIONS

Creating the center

1 Gather about thirty pieces of raffia with all the ends approximately in the same place. Hold them in your left hand, such that when it's tightly bundled it measures approximately ⅜ inch (1 cm) wide. Add or take away strands as needed.

2 Measure a 3.5-yard (3 m) piece of linen, and feed one end through a sharp darning needle. Holding the raffia bundle in your left hand with the ends pointing to the right, align the tail of the linen with the end pointing to the left. They should be parallel to one another, overlapping 4 inches (10 cm) or so. Bring them together in one bundle. (A)

3 With the linen (the wrapping linen), begin wrapping at the far right end of the raffia bundle. Directionally, wrap away from your body and around the bigger bundle moving your wrap from right to left. (B) The wraps should be side by side and cover the entire bundle—the bundle should not be visible through the wraps. Continue wrapping until 3 inches (7.5 cm) of the bundle is covered.

4 Fold the wrapped bundle in half to make the center of the basket (C). Secure the two halves together in the following process: Bring the linen around the top bundle (D), bring the needle through the center of the two bundles from back to front. (E) Bring the linen around the lower bundle, bring the needle back through the center from back to front so the wrapping linen is ready to begin the process again wrapping the linen around the top bundle. (F) Continue this weaving work from the left to the right, towards the fold, weaving the two bundles together and creating a solid center. (G) At the fold, bury the end of your wrapping linen on the back side of your piece. (H)

5 End any wrapping piece by burying the needle and end of the wrapping linen under a number of wraps, pull through and clip the end close to the wraps. (I)

A
B
C
D
E
F
G
H
I

6 Start a new piece of wrapping linen by feeding your needle under a number of wraps on the back of the basket center with the needle coming out where you want to start wrapping from. (J) In this case, back at where the uncovered bundle of raffia exits the wrapping.

7 Cut the short ends of the raffia from the lower bundle very close to where the wrapping began. (K) Wrap an additional 1.25 to 1.5 inches (3 to 4 cm) of the top bundle so that it can coil around the center hiding the cut ends. (L)

Round 1

1 Rotate the basket clockwise so that the loose raffia bundle continues to flow to the left, and the well wrapped portion continues to keep to the right. (M) Now, bring the needle through the very center and wrap the linen around the initial bundle and the new part being wrapped. This longer wrap secures the new bundle to the bundle from the prior round (a securing wrap).

2 After the securing wrap, snugly wrap seven times around just the bundle of raffia (bundle wraps). Keep the bundle close to the center to avoid loose securing wraps. After the seven bundle wraps, complete a securing wrap around both the current bundle and the bundle from the round below. (N) Continue this process of seven bundle wraps, one securing wrap moving right to left around the full center of the basket. (O)

3 As you come around the other end of the basket, continue your securing wraps around the bundle below as well as the one you're currently wrapping. (P) Continue around in the same way to the end of the round (to the cut end of the center).

Rounds 2 though 5

1 Continue the same pattern of wrapping, collecting the round below and the round you're currently working on with each securing wrap. (Q) To keep the piece flat for now, do some of the tightening of the securing and bundle wraps while the piece is flat on the table. (R) Make sure there is enough diameter in each round of your raffia that the piece can sit flat and isn't curving up on the sides.

J
K
L
M
N
O
P
Q
R

S
T
U
V
W
X
Y
Z

Adding Raffia

1 As your raffia pieces start to shorten, you'll need to add new raffia lengths to keep the bulk of your bundle at the same ⅜-inch (1 cm) width. Add raffia by adding a piece to the bundle with the tail extending beyond where you just wrapped. (S) Continue the wrapping pattern encasing the new piece of raffia as you go. (T) After a number of wraps, go back to the tail and clip it off as close to the basket as you can. (U) Throughout the bowl, add pieces of raffia as needed to keep your bundle full and even at the ⅜-inch (1 cm) size. At some point, you will need to add pieces as you get to the end of your typical raffia length. (V)

Rounds 6 through 8

1 Start to form a bowl shape beginning with Round 6. Do this by bringing the bundle up a tad on the prior round as you wrap. (W) Some of this happens naturally as you hold and make the bowl. Manage the positions of the sides as you are wrapping to form the desired shape.

Round 9—Creating the handle

1 Wrap around about five-sixths of the round. At the corner of the bowl, create a handle by securing the coil with eight securing wraps in a row. (X) This provides extra stability for the handle as well as a decorative detail. Next, wrap the coil freely for approximately 3 inches (7.5 cm). (Y) Form a handle shape and secure the coil with eight securing wraps 2 inches (5 cm) further along the bowl. (Z)

Finishing the Bowl

1 Cut the remaining raffia at an angle with about 1 inch (2.5 cm) remaining in length. (AA) Angle the remaining raffia down the side of the bowl. Continue to wrap around the raffia, securing each wrap into the bowl behind the raffia bundle, until the tail end of the raffia is fully covered. (BB) Weave your linen tail into the back of the wrapped ending to finish. Clip or cover any errant raffia or linen ends. (CC)

AA

BB

CC

Anne Weil believes that everyone can make beautiful things. Her goal is to design and create simple, elegant, and accessible craft projects for all. Anne always had a passion for creation but in 2010, after close to two decades working in investment banking, she wanted to rediscover her creative voice. Anne started her blog Flax & Twine, writing how-tos and photographing her craft projects for readers. After years of sharing her projects online—and in print magazines such as *Martha Stewart*, *TapRoot*, *Domino*, and *Elle DECOR*, among others—Anne authored two books: *Knitting Without Needles* and *Weaving Within Reach*. Anne has since expanded Flax & Twine to provide carefully sourced fibers and tools to make knitting, crocheting, weaving, and basket-making easier and more enjoyable for everyone. She has also developed a line of DIY kits that come complete with everything both beginners and seasoned crafters need to create something beautiful: natural fibers, all required accessories, detailed instructions, and step-by-step videos. Today, Flax & Twine products, including kits, fibers, and tools, are available at over 500 retailers worldwide. Follow Anne's creative journey and find inspiration at @flaxandtwine on Instagram, Pinterest, TikTok, and Facebook.

FURTHER READING AND RESOURCES

Books

Albers, Josef. *The Interaction of Color,*– 50th Anniversary Edition. Yale University Press, 2013

Bayles, David, and Ted Orland. *Art & Fear*. Souvenir Press, 2008

Cerruti, Courtney, *One Color a Day Sketchbook: A Daily Art Practice*. Harry N. Abrams, 2020

Finlay, Victoria. *Color: A Natural History of the Palette*. Random House, 2004

Greene, Robert, *Mastery*. Penguin Books, 2012.

Hanisch, Carol, *The Personal is Political, http://www.carolhanisch.org/CHwritings/PIP.html*

Korn, Peter, *Why We Make Things and Why It Matters*. Random House, 2015.

Lorde, Audre, *The Masters Tools Will Never Dismantle The Master's House*. PENGUIN UK, 2018

Molesworth, Helen, *Work Ethic*. Penn State University Press, 2003

Parker, Rozsika. *The Subversive Stitch: Embroidery and the Making of the Feminine*. Bloomsbury Visual Arts, Reprint edition, 2019

Yanagi, Soetsu, *The Unknown Craftsman*. Kodansha International Ltd, 1978

Film

Handmade Nation by Faythe Levine—https://www.faythelevine.com/untitled-g6wd8

General Art Materials and Craft Supplies

If you're looking for alternatives to mega online retailers and big-box stores, here are some great places to start:

A Verb for Keeping Warm - https://www.averbforkeepingwarm.com

Blick - https://www.dickblick.com

Case for Making - https://caseformaking.com

Cheap Joes - https://cheapjoes.com

Dharma Trading - https://www.dharmatrading.com

Gallo Paints - https://agallocolors.com

Kremer Paints - https://shop.kremerpigments.com/us/

St. Louis Art Supplies - https://shop.stlartsupply.com

ACKNOWLEDGMENTS

Thanks first and foremost to Bridget Watson Payne and Jenny Wapner for seeing this as a worthy endeavor and for inviting me on board.

Thanks to each and every contributor to this book. Your professionalism, your enthusiasm, your willingness to take on a project in a color we chose for you is so appreciated. Not only do I adore all the beautiful and meaningful things you made, I cherish the inspiration, friendship, and sheer delight I feel when I think about you as humans and friends.

Thanks to my family. My kiddo who astounds me with their smarts and compassion. My husband who has helped create a home and the space where I am afforded the luxury to do the work that most compels me. My parents who always jump in to save the day, lend ears to listen, and steadfastly offer unconditional love and support. I love you all in a way that there are not adequate words in any language to express.

To all of the early art/craft folks who met online with blogs and flickr in the nostalgic era pre-algorithm (and in no particular order): Risa Friedman, Wendy Crabb, Blair Stocker, Eireann Lorsung, Eling Chang, Aurora Robson, Christine Castro Hughes, Heather Smith Jones, Betsy Thompson, Bri Drennon, Jen McGee, Jan Halvarson, Shari Altman, Andrea Jenkins, Andrea Lampman, Cyndi Monaghan, Mati McDonough, Gwen Shlichta, Kerstin Svenson, Amisha Sharma, Martha McQuade, Emily Demsky, Tania Skevos, Jenna Park, Anne Bowerman, Gracia and Louise, Amy Karol, Nichole Ramirez, Tracy Bartley, Melissa Franz, Natalie Tweedie, Susan Schwake, Lisa Congdon, Camilla Engman, and I'm sure I'm missing many, but all you too. THANKS for being the people who read my first musings on the meaning of art and craft for me and helped me figure out I maybe wasn't going to figure this all out, but to keep going anyway.

To Susie Ghahremani—my forever wordsmith and twin. To Kim Austin—one of the most inherently supportive and lovely people on the planet. To Connie Begg—who is a great listener and a validator of all the things grad school. To Vilasinee Bunnag—whose food tastes and politics and humor always get me. I can't thank you enough for your wisdom and friendships.

To Katherine Sherwood, Hung Liu, Ron Nagle, Mary Lovelace O'Neal, Richard Shaw, George Miyasaki, Kevin Radly, Grace Munakata—thanks for being my teachers and mentors and for showing me what artists do, how they think. You all helped mold me into the artist I am today. To Walter Maciel and Jake Martinez—the literal support you show for my work and the trust and love and care is just so beyond. I am forever grateful.

To the memories of my grandparents Shirley and Sidney—without you I would not make the things I do. And to Rori—I miss you.

And finally, to all my artist and maker friends, the ones who I share secrets with and the ones who I only see on the socials and internets: this book is for you. For *us*. May we always toggle between art and craft and find the voice to make the things that live in our heads and hearts.

INDEX

Hardie Grant North America
2912 Telegraph Ave
Berkeley, CA 94705
hardiegrant.com

Published in the United States by Hardie Grant North America, an imprint of Hardie Grant Publishing Pty Ltd.

Library of Congress Cataloging-in-Publication Data is available upon request.

ISBN: 9781964786049
ISBN: 9781964786056 (eBook)

Printed in CHINA
Design by Brooke Johnson
First Edition

in fog
freshly cut
deepest petals